# THE AUTOBIOGRAPHY OF HOSEA STOUT

EDITED BY
REED A. STOUT

◆

REVISED BY
STEPHEN L. PRINCE

THE UNIVERSITY OF UTAH PRESS
UTAH STATE HISTORICAL SOCIETY
*Salt Lake City*

First published in the *Utah Historical Quarterly*, volume 30, numbers 1, 2, 3 and 4.
Copyright © 1962 by the Utah State Historical Society.

 The Defiance House Man colophon is a registered trademark of the
University of Utah Press. It is based upon a four-foot-tall, Ancient
Puebloan pictograph (late PIII) near Glen Canyon, Utah.

14 13 12 11 10      1 2 3 4 5

LIBRARY OF CONGRESS CATALOGING-IN-PUBLICATION DATA
Stout, Hosea, 1810-1889.
The autobiography of Hosea Stout / edited by Reed A. Stout ; edited and revised by Stephen L.
Prince.
      p.   cm.
"First published in the Utah historical quarterly, volume 30, numbers 1, 2, 3, and 4 ... 1962"—T.p.
verso.
   Includes bibliographical references.
   ISBN 978-0-87480-957-2 (paper : alk. paper)
   1. Stout, Hosea, 1810-1889. 2. Mormon pioneers—Utah—Biography. 3. Frontier and pio-
neer life—Utah. 4. Mormons—Utah—Biography. 5. Legislators—Utah—Biography. 6. Mormon
Church—Utah—History—19th century. 7. Mormon Church—Illinois—Nauvoo—History—19th
century. 8. Utah—History—19th century. 9. Nauvoo (Ill.)—History—19th century. I. Stout, Reed
A. II. Prince, Stephen L., 1946- III. Utah State Historical Society. IV. Title.
   F826.S76A3 2010
   328.73'092—dc22
   [B]

                                                                        2010007657

Printed and bound by Sheridan Books, Inc., Ann Arbor, Michigan.

# Contents

INTRODUCTION BY STEPHEN L. PRINCE ◆ vii

INTRODUCTION TO THE 1962 EDITION BY REED A. STOUT ◆ xi

AUTOBIOGRAPHY OF HOSEA STOUT 1810 TO 1835 ◆ 1

AUTOBIOGRAPHY OF HOSEA STOUT 1810 TO 1844 ◆ 55

NOTES ◆ 61

# Map

AREA OF EARLY YEARS OF HOSEA STOUT ◆ FACING PAGE 1

# Introduction by Stephen L. Prince

Before his diaries were discovered, Hosea Stout was a relatively obscure figure in Mormon history. "His name turned up consistently in Mormon annals," wrote Dale L. Morgan in his review of the published diary in the *Utah Historical Quarterly*, "but none of the standard biographical works contained a notice of him, and what manner of person he was, few could have guessed." Though accurate, Morgan's statement was remarkable considering the important roles Stout played in early Mormon history.

Hosea Stout, while already serving as clerk of the Nauvoo High Council, was chosen to be the "recorder" or clerk of the fledgling Nauvoo Legion, and in that capacity penned all written records of the legion's early organizational meetings. He rose in the ranks of the legion and was promoted to acting brigadier general following the assassination of Joseph and Hyrum Smith. Shortly afterwards he was made captain of police at Nauvoo, guarding church leaders and the city from the threatening mob. In that position he directed the first crossings of the Mississippi River during the exodus from Nauvoo; he subsequently also headed police work at Winter Quarters.

Arriving in Utah in 1848, Hosea acted as Brigham Young's attorney and became the first attorney general for the Territory of Utah. He was a member of the Utah Territorial Legislature, and from 1856 to 1857 was speaker of the House of Representatives. He was a regent for the University of Deseret and a judge advocate of the Nauvoo Legion in Utah; in 1862 he was appointed United States District Attorney for the Territory of Utah by President Abraham Lincoln. Also in 1862, he was sent to southern Utah as a member of the "Cotton Mission," where he served as St. George's first city attorney as well as president of the St. George High

Council. In 1867 he returned to Salt Lake City, where he promptly became the city attorney, and in 1881 he capped his career by being elected (at the age of 71) to a final two-year term in the Utah House of Representatives.

Most of the aforementioned occurred after Hosea commenced his diary in October 1844 and to a great extent is described in great detail in the diary. Fortunately, he also wrote two autobiographies that together tell much of his personal story during his earlier years. The first was written in 1845 for the Eleventh Quorum of Seventies in Nauvoo, Illinois. Curiously, Hosea chose to write that record impersonally, as if writing about someone else. Because it covers a later time period than does his other, later, autobiography, it is referred to as his "second autobiography." Because it was likely written as a sort of church assignment, the record touches only briefly on the years before he became acquainted with and was baptized a member of the Church of Jesus Christ of Latter-day Saints. While giving a rather detailed account of the conflict between Mormons and Missourians in Caldwell County, Missouri, particularly of the Battle of Crooked River, he wrote the story of his years in Nauvoo almost in outline form, scarcely venturing into any detail.

Far more illuminating and satisfying is the autobiography written while at Winter Quarters on the banks of the Missouri River during the winter of 1846 to 1847. As Dale Morgan wrote, it is "possessed of such artless simplicity and charms as to be one of the great personal documents of our literature." That story begins with his Quaker ancestors, giving an account of their early history and their movement from Pennsylvania to North Carolina, Tennessee, and Kentucky, where Hosea was born in 1810. Financial misfortune led his father to place his children in the care of a Shaker community at Pleasant Hill, Kentucky, just a few miles from their home. The four years that Hosea spent among the Shakers doubtlessly provided a religious foundation that greatly influenced the direction of his life and may well have contributed to basic beliefs that facilitated his later conversion to Mormonism.

In the autobiography Hosea recounts being reunited with his family and moving to a Quaker community in Ohio, where he identified with that religion. Heartbroken after the death of his mother, Hosea was shaken to his core when his father abandoned him, though happily he was rescued by the goodness of a few Quaker men, including one of his uncles; subsequently he removed to the Illinois prairie in 1828, settling in a community founded by another uncle. There he continued his religious journey, first by joining the Methodists and subsequently investigating Mormonism.

Hosea Stout commenced writing the autobiography in February 1847 while hunkered down at Winter Quarters on the Nebraska side of the Missouri River; in it he wrote his life story to 1835, and then he laid down his pen. Though it is thought that he intended to complete the work, nothing more ever was written and for many years Hosea remained one of the lesser-known figures in nineteenth-century Mormon history. That changed somewhat after the several volumes of his diary were brought together, expertly edited by Juanita Brooks, and jointly published in 1964 by the University of Utah Press and the Utah State Historical Society. *On the Mormon Frontier: The Diary of Hosea Stout, 1844–1889,* in Morgan's words, provided "one of the most magnificent windows upon Mormon history ever opened." Thereafter Stout's name appeared in numerous volumes and articles concerning Mormon as well as western American history, though typically it is associated only with quotations from his diary.

A few years before the publication of the diary, Hosea Stout's autobiographies were edited by Reed Stout, one of his great-grandsons, and published in serial form in 1962 in the *Utah Historical Quarterly.* Although *On the Mormon Frontier* was reprinted in 1982 and again in 2009, Hosea's autobiographies languished in relative obscurity. In consideration of a forthcoming biography of Hosea Stout, the University of Utah Press again reprinted *On the Mormon Frontier,* this time in a single-volume paperback edition.

Though Reed Stout did a fine job of editing the autobiographies in 1962, a half century of scholarship, not to mention information much more easily accessed in the digital age, led to a decision to publish a revised edition. The text remains exactly as written by Hosea Stout and printed in 1962 in the *Utah Historical Quarterly.* More than thirty footnotes have been added for this edition. In addition, minor corrections have been made to a few footnotes and some details have been added to others. Particularly in the second autobiography, several very lengthy footnotes have been abridged to make them more accessible to the reader.

# Introduction to the 1962 edition by Reed Stout

Few people have had a greater sense of history than the Mormons of the middle nineteenth century. Possibly none have been more disposed than they to make a day to day record and chronicle of their experiences, thoughts, and observations.

That this is so is quite understandable in view of the early Mormon certainty that they were living in a period of apocalypse. To them, the heavens were again opened after being closed for almost two thousand years. Man was once more in communication with God, and a prophet was again on earth receiving the word and the will of the Lord. The divine church was in process of being restored, and the holy priesthood, long ago taken from man, was being returned. Events were preparing the world for the second coming of Christ. Miracles and heavenly manifestations were commonplace. In such a period it was only natural that whatever reasons men have even in ordinary times to keep diaries and write memoirs would compel these early Mormons to record the exciting and stirring things they were seeing and doing.

But perhaps even more important in giving these early Mormons a feeling of history and a reason for keeping journals and records, were the examples and instructions of their leaders. Their prophet, Joseph Smith, kept a daily journal, and in the earliest days of the Church of Jesus Christ of Latter-day Saints, he instructed his chief lieutenant, Oliver Cowdery, to act as historian and recorder.[1] Other church leaders likewise kept daily journals. Early in the year 1831, just a few months after the church was organized, the keeping of official records was given a divine stamp of approval when Joseph Smith announced a revelation calling John

Whitmer to be church historian "to keep the church record and history continually."[2] Not only did Joseph Smith see to it that persons in authority in the church kept regular records of their own, but he also urged the ordinary rank and file of the church to do the same.

With the murder of Joseph Smith and his brother Hyrum June 27, 1844, the leadership of the church passed to the Quorum of Twelve Apostles and its president, Brigham Young. The keeping of records and writing of journals received added stress and impetus under this leadership. Willard Richards was appointed church historian, and he and other of the authorities labored day after day compiling a history of the church. Committees were designated in Nauvoo to write histories of various organizations of the Mormon people and events in the life of the church. In the priesthood quorums each member was urged to prepare his own biography as part of a regular quorum project. As the Mormons evacuated their city of Nauvoo in 1846 to escape a growing storm of hostility and as their exodus to the valley of the Great Salt Lake got under way, they were given specific instruction by their leaders, "Let every Elder keep a journal…"[3]

So, whether because of a natural tendency man has to keep diaries or because of the examples and instructions of their leaders, the early Mormons have bequeathed to us a wealth of records, journals, diaries, biographies, and personal histories. In these they have traced the days of the church as it moved from New York State, through Ohio, and on to Jackson and Caldwell counties in Missouri, and then to Nauvoo, Illinois. In greater measure, they have chronicled their struggles from Nauvoo through the snow, rain, and mud, past the way-stations of Garden Grove, Mt. Pisgah, and Kanesville, Iowa and Winter Quarters, Nebraska. And in even more abundance they have pictured the minutiae of daily pioneer life in their diaries and histories as the Saints (as the Mormons called themselves) rolled in covered wagons, pushed handcarts through the heat of summer and bitter cold of winter over the prairies to the Rocky Mountains, and as they established their homes in the Great Basin. Historians, reviewing the writings of the early Mormons, have marveled at the persistence and tenacity with which they combined the writing of their journals and histories with the privations of pioneer life.

Among the most persevering and thorough of the early Mormon diarists was Hosea Stout. His journal commencing in 1844 and continuing until 1866 provides a vivid picture by a keen observer of critical periods in the history of the Mormon people and their church. As chief of police in Nauvoo, clerk of the high council, and colonel and acting brigadier-general of the Nauvoo Legion, he was an active participant in the period of confusion in Nauvoo following the murder of Joseph Smith and in the subsequent conflict leading to the abandonment of the city. He and the police directed the first crossings of the Mississippi River from Nauvoo. His detailed descriptions of the crossings and the hardships of the journey of the advance parties of Saints across Iowa to Winter Quarters are unmatched by any account heretofore published.

As an on-the-spot observer, clerk of the high council, and captain of police at Winter Quarters, Hosea Stout chronicled in his journals the turmoil of establishing a temporary home for thousands of refugees; the task of providing protection against marauding Indians; the jealousies, bickerings, and falling away by many of the Saints from the church; and the preparations for the journey on to the Rocky Mountains. While not a member of the first pioneer group to enter the valley of the Great Salt Lake, Hosea led an expedition west from Winter Quarters for the relief of the band under Brigham Young returning in the fall of 1847 from the Great Basin. Moving from Winter Quarters to Salt Lake City in 1848, he acted as attorney for Brigham Young and was appointed attorney general for the territory of Utah. In these capacities and as regent for the University of Deseret, judge advocate of the Nauvoo Legion, member of the territorial legislature, publisher of an early newspaper, and as an interested participant, Hosea Stout observed and recorded from day to day the details of early pioneer life, conflict with the federal government, and the growth of an empire in the Great Basin.

The Stout journals, except for a portion in the library of the Historian of the Church of Jesus Christ of Latter-day Saints covering a period of a few months, are in the library of the Utah State Historical Society in Salt Lake City. In addition to the journals there exist two autobiographies, one at the Historical Society, the other at the LDS Historian's library. Typescripts have been made of the journals and the autobiographies, and these have been deposited in several libraries across the United States. In these libraries, the journals and autobiographies have received the attention of students and writers dealing with western and Mormon history and have been extensively quoted.[4]

Recognizing the importance of the Hosea Stout journals and the interest that would be given them if made available for more general circulation, the Utah State Historical Society is now engaged in having them prepared for publication under the editorship of Mrs. Juanita Brooks,[5] well-known writer in the field of western and Mormon history. Since the autobiographies are likely to be of as much interest to some scholars as the journals themselves, they will appear in this and following issues of the *Quarterly*.

The autobiographies provide an introduction to the journals and touch upon subjects of interest in the early history of Kentucky, the Shaker religion and life in their communities, incidents in southeastern Ohio and central Illinois during the early part of the nineteenth century, the religious fervor on the frontier during this period, the Black Hawk War, and events and references to persons in the earliest days of the Mormon Church.

During the winter of 1846–47, the first autobiography was written by Hosea Stout at Winter Quarters on the banks of the Missouri River, where the Saints were stationed after their crossing of Iowa from Nauvoo to prepare for the coming move to establish their homes in the Rocky Mountains. At the time he was writing this autobiography, Hosea was perhaps mindful that Brigham Young a short time before had instructed him to continue his daily journal because the period through which the Mormons were then passing would be among the most important in the history of the world.

Until February 6, 1847, Hosea Stout and his family lived at Winter Quarters in a tent, the same tent he had lived in for a year since he first pitched it on the west bank of the Mississippi River after leaving Nauvoo. After that date he lived in a log house built by himself, which he describes as "12 feet square on the outside." In these cramped quarters, but protected from the cold, wind, and snow encountered while on patrol duty, and after the minutes of the high council of which he was clerk were written, Hosea Stout went to work on his autobiography.[6]

The first autobiography covering the period 1810 to 1835 was written in a notebook 6 ¼ x 3 ¾ and three fourths inches in size. After continuing in considerable detail for 125 pages, the narrative abruptly ends. That Hosea Stout intended to continue is manifest from his statement in the next to last sentence in the autobiography in which he refers to his purchase of a mill seat that resulted in a lawsuit "as will be hereafter seen." Certainly the promise of a further statement regarding the lawsuit is inconsistent with his discontinuance of the autobiography. Possibly, however, the press of duties of pioneer life, the preparation for the move to the Rocky Mountains, and the time required to keep up his daily journal prevented further work on the autobiography.

The second autobiography written by Hosea Stout in 1845 for the Eleventh Quorum of Seventies in Nauvoo, Illinois, is much shorter than the first and touches briefly upon the period covered in the first. However, where the first autobiography ends in 1835, the second continues until 1844. Herein Hosea describes his move from Illinois to Missouri to join the Mormons in Caldwell County where he participated in the conflicts between Mormons and Missourians. After the battle of Crooked River, Hosea recounts his flight from Missouri and other events leading to the period in his life when his journal begins on October 4, 1844.

The narrative here appearing is exactly as written by Hosea Stout as he sat in his small log cabin over a century ago. Original spelling, grammar, and punctuation have been retained.

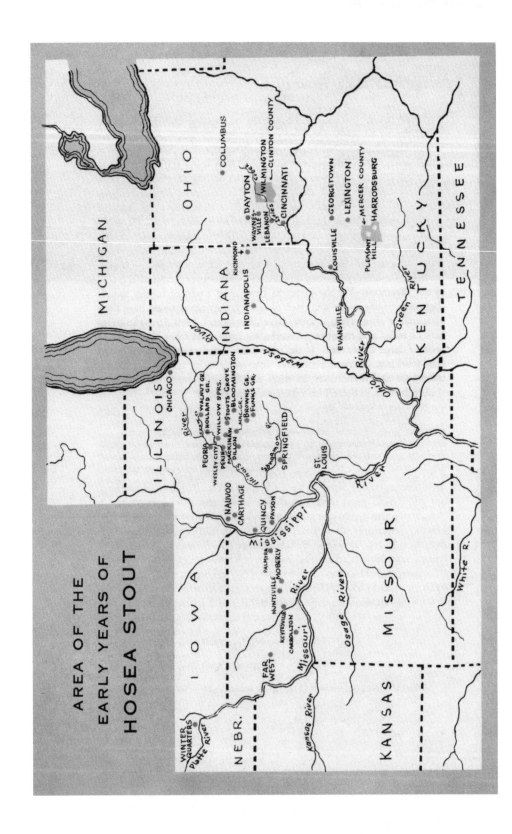

AREA OF THE
EARLY YEARS OF
HOSEA STOUT

# Autobiography of Hosea Stout

## 1810 TO 1835

In giving the history of ones life it is necessary also that a person should give a short account of his ancestors; which I will do and also something about my fathers family and the family of my mother.

My grandfather,[1] who was a quaker, resided in North-Carolina, Oxford County, where also my father was born [June 25, 1773],[2] and raised untill he was about sixteen or seventeen years of age. About that time my grandfather, after loosing nearly all his property by lawsuits, and family removed to East Tennessee, where they lived untill my father was about twenty-five years of age. My father then went back to North Carolina to the house of my grandmother, who was a widow, by the name of Pleasant Smith,[3] who was also a Quaker. She was an aunt to my father that is his mother's sister. She had five daughters and two sons. Her daughters names are Esther, Anna, Abigail, Sarah, & Rebecca. Her sons names are Thomas and Daniel. They were but boys when my father came there. He staid there one summer and raised a crop with them and in the fall he was married [November 3, 1798] to her daughter Anna.

Now the widow was not well pleased with them, for they ran away and was married contrary to the rules of their society, which thing is esteemed a sin among the Quakers, and will excommunicate one from their society if they do not make satisfaction. Nor could they do any other way for my father had been previously cut off from their Church for enlisting in the army.[4] However they came home again & was received by my grandmother.

Shortly after my father & mother removed to East Tennessee where they stayed till they had five children namely Rebecca [1799?], Sarah [1800], Samuel [1802], Mary & Margaret [1804]. The two latter were twins, and the two boys [Samuel and Daniel] died when they were very young. They then moved to Madison County Kentucky and there remained untill they had two children more namely Anna [1806] and Daniel [1808] they then removed to Mercer County,[5] [Kentucky, where] Myself Cynthia [1812] and Joseph Allen [December 5, 1815] was born. (I was born September 18th 1810) Cynthia died when she was but 4 or five years old. He [my father] lived near a Shaker[6] Village called Pleasant Hill when I was born. About or a little after Cynthia was born he [my father] had bad luck, from sickness and other misfortunes, which quite discouraged him; and indu[c] ed him to put his children out. The Shakers, finding he was inclined to let them go, came and influenced him to let them have them, to go to school, accordingly all his children were taken by them.[7] My brother Joseph Allen was not yet born.

My Sister Rebecca was, at this time about sixteen or seventeen years old. It was in the Spring of the year 1814. She, I think, joined them from her own free will and accord, and remained with them untill she died. She was, ever from the time she joined them, a firm believer in their faith & doctrine and became an influentual and worthy "Sister" among them, one on whom they bestowed their greatest confidence and was appointed what they call a "Deaconess"[8] who have the charge and superintendence of work of the "Sisters". She died about the year 1825 of the consumption. The first year we were there my Sister Cynthia died. About three years after we went there [about 1817] my Sister Sally [Sarah] left them and went home to my father's house.

After we went there we were separated, as is their custom. The boys are taken & classed with a family[9] of boys of their own age, and the girls are taken and like-wise classed with girls of their own age;[10] each class was put under the superintendence of one or more "Sisters" acording as the number may require.

After the boys became larger, say, seven or eight, they were taken and put under the care of one or two men. I was first put under the care of two women with the smallest class of boys; but the man, who had the charge of the larger boys had also the oversight of us, to see that we might be kept in proper subjection, least we might become to unruly for the "Sisters." I had not been there long before I was called upon to "confess my sins." I had been, previous to this, allowed to, run almost at large, to go where I pleased & make as much noise as I saw proper, which was not allowable with those who were diciplined and brought under the rigor of their rules. They had however excelent rules for the government of their children They were not allowed to fight and quarrel nor have any disputation among themselves. In playing they were not allowed to make much noise, nor go only on certain prescribed premises; and a transgression of these rules were a sin which we had to confess, which we always did; we were afraid not to do it least the "bad man" should get us; and if this was not enough we were still afraid least some one of our comerades would betray us, and then we would come under the displeasure of the Mistress, and also, be in danger of going to the "Bad place" which place was often held up to us in a most aggravated sense. I have sat and trembled for myself while hearing this awful place described, by them, to my young mind.

These rules were necessary to keep a large company of boys in proper subordination. Perhaps I may say more of their instructions and rules as I go along: but to return to my subject. At the time I was called upon "to confess" I was playing with some other little Shaker boys and while I was passing by a house a man, by the name of John Shane,[11] who had the superintendence of the larger class of boys, and consequently over me too, called me into the house, and asked me if I did not think it was time I had confessed my sins. This embarrassed me, I told him I did not know. However I knew very well what he ment. He then had me confess. I do not now recollect what I did confess. I remember that he asked me if that was all. I told him it was. He, then, let me go and join my comrades again. From this time I had, as also all the rest of the boys, to confess our sins every night,[12] so strict were we taught to confess the truth & tell all that we had done, that was wrong, that I have known them sometimes to get up out of their beds and confess things which they had forgotten: not daring to let it go till the next night for fear they might die and the "Bad man" would get them. We would scroupulously tell all we had said or done through the day that was not according to the rules laid down, though it might cause us to get a severe reprimand and sometimes a moderate flogging.

I staid a considerable length of time in this class, but I do not know how long.

While living here my little sister Cynthia died [December 4, 1815] & I well remember seeing the funeral concourse of people marching to her burial.

From this place we were removed to another part of the village and put under the care and instructions of two Sisters by the names of Nelly Flemmings and Maria Sailor,[13] if I mistake not.

In a house adjoining, to the one in which we were put, was a larger class of boys, who were from about 8 to 16 years of age.

They were under the care of a man named Anthony Dunlavy,[14] who also had the oversight of us. But he never administered in this part of his office only when some of us were too unruly for the women.

Here we had something to do besides play. There were, I think, about 20 maybe 30 of us.

We were now learned how to brade straw for hats. Those in this class were from 4 to 8 years of age and some of this class were lately brought in from the country and entirely undiciplined.

It was astonishing to see the work we done.

While at our work, we were seated on long benches, as in a school, and each one had his task to do, which he generally done.

I have known some of them to move the mark (a piece of straw tied around their brade) on their brade and thus get his task done a long time before the rest of us

But he was sure to be detected For when he should have braded enough for a hat, it would be all examined and measured over again and if he had cheated he was sure to be severely punished for his dishonesty.

The usual methods of punishment, which those two women used with us, were whipping, making us stay in the house in play time, and sometimes brade in the mean time, putting us under the floor in a little dark hole dug out for the purpose of putting roots &c in to keep them from the frost.

While there, if this did not humble us enough, they would frighten us with horid stories about the "Bad man" coming and catching us.

I have been almost scared out of my wits while in this dark and dreary place and would make any kind of a promise they would demand to be liberated and so would almost all the rest.

I shall never forget one time when one of the most obstinate boys was frightned into submission. He had been whiped about the time we were going to bed and would not hush crying.

They in vain attempted to stop him untill at length they told him if he did not hush they would call in the Bad man who would carry him away.

He still continued to ball louder than ever, while some of the rest of us were in great suspense least he might thus bring the old gentleman on to us. At len[g]th one of the women went to the door and commenced calling. Our fears increasing at the same time.

In a few minutes we heard a loud gruff surley voice demand what was wanting, to which she replied there was a bad boy who would not mind her & she wanted him to take him away to the bad place (hell) He then called quite loud for the boy who was still crying and did not stop untill she commenced pulling him out of bed.

This was Dunlavy who had altered his voice.

This left an impressive lessen on our minds and made us more ready to mind

When we first heard the old man speak, we covered up our heads (for we had just gone to bed) and lay trembling least we should be all carried away together.

Such stories as these were continually impressed upon our minds and such was my ideas of the "Bad Man" being around my bed of night that I have often lain trembling with fear, not daring to move, and imagined that I could see him ready to take me "of[f] to his dark hole"

But now for the subject again:

After we had done brading we were allowed to go and play awhile and then come in and larn our books. It was here that my young idea was first "taught to shoot." I here learned my letters & soon after learned to spell.

The times for our lessons, our brading, & our play, was judiciously arrainged, not kept at either long enough to weary us.

I consider the regulations good and well adapted to keep a large number of boys in subjection.

In the morning when we get up after washing and performing our morning devotional services, which was by singing and dancing

The "Sisters" under whose care we were would sing a Shaker song and all the boys dance. At certain parts of the song, we had to run around in a circle, sometimes also clapping our hands, shouting, & making a great noise & uproar.

The like performances were gone through in the evening.

Always at meal time, when seated around the table, before we commenced eating, we had to kneel down and shut our eyes about one minute then all rising up at the same time, would take our seats again and commence eating

While eating we were not allowed to speak unless spoken to, by those who waited on the table.

We were taught when we wanted any thing though it was from the smallest person, to ask them to do it "if they would be so kind", and after they had done it, the person would say, "I thank you kindly". To which the other answers "you are kindly welcome", and such like civilities in all cases were punctually observed.

I have often thought if fathers and those who have the charge of families would adopt some of their rules and mode of dicipline, it would be a great improvement to their peace and social happiness. Thus having good order and quietude instead of a continual scene of disobedience bickering, strife, quarrelling, contradicting each other, bad language backbiting, and the like, and an eternal rotine of ill manners, bad conduct &c. the example being allways set by the parents or guardian.

But now for the subject again

The first time that ever I remember seeing my brother Joseph Allen was while living here.[15]

My mother used to come to see me and bring him along with her.

She would bring apples and other little articles to please me.

I remember that she took me out doors once, to have a talk with me & gave me an apple telling me to be a good boy, and had me to eat there, least the other boys might get it away from me. I reluctantly went out with her and was in a hurry to go in again, least the boys might think I loved her, for we were taught to spurn the idea of paternal affection. I did not yet realize the kind hand of maternal affection that was want to administer to me but deprived of the privelege only in this clandestine way.

We were moved from this place to another part of the village & there put under the sole care of Anthony Dunlavy & James Davis

Here we had more priviledes only We were kept at our books and other employments, as they saw proper from time to time.

While here I learned to read tollerably well.

On the 21st day of August 1818, (on the Sabbath) some of the boys told me that my father was coming ("Old Jo. Stout" as we called him) whereupon I ran and hid but Dunlavy made me come back. It was while the Shakers were gone to meeting.

He told Dunlavy that he had come after me to go and stay a week with my mother as she was very anxious to see me.

Dunlavy, aware of his intentions, would not consent.[16]

They had a long talk but to no purpose. In the minetime I went off to play rolling a hoop, & still holding on to it slowly.

At length my father came to me and endeavoured to pursuade me to go But I refused, all his arguments had no effect on me.

After both of us returned to the house, Dunlavy still refusing my father picked me up and set me on his shoulder and walked off with me.

I screamed and cried as loud as I could; and tried to get away but, in vain. My nois soon aroused the whole place and out came the "Sisters," screaming crying and begging him to let me go. There was no resistance offered by the men, it being contrary to their faith.[17] Had there been any, they might have easily prevented him & rescued me.

Among the rest of the women were my own sisters who were more earnest than the rest for having me retained.

He Stopped a while to expostulate and told them that he would bring me back next Sabbath, but this done no good towards satisfying, so he went off with me.

I had been taught that the "worldlings" had nothing to eat and if I left them, [the Shakers, I] would starve so when my father started away with me I was frightened because I did not expect to live untill next Sunday, and thought that my doom was sealed and I must surely die. As he was travelling along I took particular notice of every thing I passed & viewed the situation of the country intending to run away the first chance.

At length we passed through a low bottom of sugar maple where the dark gloom which overshadowed me, caused such a lonesome & solitary feeling as I viewed this dark cool, damp, "wildering maze, as I sat on his shoulder & the cobwebs drawing over my face that I gave up the last & my lingering ferlorn hope of escape for I was affraid to pass alone through this trackless, and dismal forest

I had never before been in a thick forrest like that.

My last hope had now f[l]ed, to starve was inevitable now & I was almost in despair and began to weep and wail my unhappy fate. But my father assured me that I should not die but have plenty to eat and return next sunday. But I did not believe him. So strong had the impression been made on my mind that the "worldlings" did not have enough to keep them from starving allmost & sometimes to death.

At length we arrived at home, where I met with my mother, Sister Sarah & brother Joseph Allen, all who were very glad to see me, But to me it was no joy, for the fear of starving still lingered within me, and I felt more like a condemned criminal than a son just returning to the sweet embraces of an affectionate and doating mother.

My father at this time was tending a mill for Robert Reagan on Shaw[n]ee Run creek, some four or five miles from Pleasant hill & perhaps as far from the junction of that stream with the Kentucky river He lived in an adjoining room to the mill.

I had not been there but a few hours, before I went to play with my brother, and in throwing stones in the mill dam, I unthoughtedly hollowed, and was immediately, so consience smitten at that transgression that I stopped my sport a few minutes and finally resolved that I would remember & confess it when I returned to Pleasant Hill the next Sunday. So strictly scrupulous was I to obey the instructions of my Shaker tutors. In the afternoon my father and all the family went down the creek to amuse me by fishing I thought this a most flagrant violation of the law of God, and, although well amused, was still afraid of the consequences but comforted myself with a determination to confess all, when I returned next Sunday and this satisfied or lulled my conscience.

After we returned home several of the neighbours came in to see me. All with one accord endeavoured to turn me against the "Shakers. Among the rest was a Mr. Lee, who came swaggering along half drunk & commenced praising me & telling me what a fine boy I was giving me as he spoke a dollar in silver and wanted me to say if I would not leave the Shakers, to which I consented to do, as I became now convinced that they were my friends & were kind to me and would not kill me nor starve me to death as I had been taught. I began to think the Shakers had taught me wrong & first gave up the idea of confessing my sins any more & in a few hours more was entirely converted over to the ways of the world and at dark was perfectly turned against the Shakers and would have abhored the idea of going back any more.

A new scene of things now had to be entered into. Being now out of the reach of Shaker dicipline & having no sins to confess, no boys to tell on me, but all willing to hide every mean trick, I soon was well initiated into all the rude mischief which the white, black, and yellow customers of a large mill & distillery could bring forth and went forth and acted in all cases perfectly free and uncounscience-bound and had now only to seek to keep it from my parents & no fears of the "Bad-Man"

My mother paid strict attention to my education and kept me at my book more or less every day, and I was sure to have a lessen to studdy every time I was caught in mischief.

During the winter my uncle Ephraim Stout[18] and his sone, Ephraim, came to see us from Misssouri. They were on a general visit to see all his brothers & sisters. They remained there some time and while there he induced my father to move to Ohio to my uncle Isaac Stout[19] Accordingly in the following spring he [my father] started, and stopped [on the way to Ohio] about one week in the edge of Pleasant Hill. Here I had an opportunity of seeing my four sisters [Rebecca, Mary, Margaret, and Anna] and old playmates again, all who earnestly endeavoured to induce me to come back and live with them; but I was now as much averse to them as I was to the worldings last fall when I was taken away

I even scorned the idea of being called a Shaker boy.

We passed through Lexington & I think Georgetown and crossed the Ohio river at Cincinnatti and from thence to Lebanon, and arrived at my uncles in Clinton County, Ohio about three miles West of Wilmington the county seat, on Lytle's Creek[20]

We were conducted to the residence of my uncle's by a man named James McVey,[21] one of his neighbours, who announced to him that we had come whereupon they all ran out to meet us in great joy & excitement. Some weeping some laughing.

My uncle Isaac came hobbling down the hill to meet us. I was astonished to see how much he resembled Anthony Dunlavy, my old Shaker tutor for he looked almost exactly like him

We stayed here perhaps three or four weeks, during which time I became very intimate with my two cousins Isaac jr. & Isaiah the latter in particular, in whose company I had great pleasure.

My father rented a farm bout one mile South from my uncle's, & we removed there & began to clear and prepare the ground for a Spring crop. My situation was now materially changed, being separated from my two cousins society, I was put to work, picking up and burning brush. This was fine sport for me at first, but I soon found that it was work, which I did not relish quite so well as playing with my cousins: but when I would not pick brush fast enough to suit my father, he would apply one to my back, as a prompter for me to put away childish things.

When summer came I was put to pulling weeds: but as soon as I was left alone would stop and go to play, which seldom failed to bring down the prompter on me when my father came: it done good however, about as long as it was in opperation, for he was no sooner gone than I was to play again.

One day, being impatient at my indolence and me arguing that I was not used to work; after giving me a severe flogging, [my father] put a chain around my neck and started away, swearing that he would "usen" me.

I supposed he was going to hang me forthwith & began to beg most lustily and promise to do better: but he went on paying no attention to me & took me out in the corn field, to a green beach tree and tied me to a long "swinging limb" and there set me to pulling up the weeds which were "in the reach of my cable tow" and went away. As soon as he was gone & I saw he had no notion of hanging me, I laid down in the shade and went to sleep soundly. The next thing I knew he had me by the chain using a beach limb as usual, swearing it was more trouble to make me work than my neck was worth.

The above is a fair specimen of my industry for several years

Sometimes I wished myself back among the Shakers, who I thought would not want me to work so hard, & if they did I would not be so solitary and alone; but knowing I could not get back, [I] would comfort myself with the idea that I would some day be "Big enough" to treat my father as he had me & to this end would try & remember all he said to me that I might return the same to him, which was no small comfort to me.

I sometimes could prevail on my mother to let my brother Allen go out to work with me, but never failed to set him at something he could not do & on his failure would most unmercifully beat & whip him and then make him promise not to tell on me, swearing if he did I would kill him the next time I got him out.

The little fellow would not know what to do. If he went with me I was sure to beat him shamefully & if he refused to go [I] would whip him for that the first oppertunity. If I chanced to mark him, I told him what to say when questioned which he never failed to do but once and was not then believed but I learned him better than to ever tell again.

Notwithstanding my tyranny and ill treatment, he always loved, feard and obeyed me & was kind & docile, ever ready to take my advice & instructions, which made me repent of my abuse to him & [I] would resolve to do so no more, which would last till he done something to displease me.

Thus passed away the summer of 1819. The first summer after I came to Ohio. In the fall my father took a place about one quarter of a mile East from here, which had belonged to my cousin Jessee Stout.[22]

Here my sister Lydia was born on the third day of January 1820.

The settlement where we now lived was Quakers as also [were] my Uncle and all my relations & we were all or nearly all who were not.

My mother had a long and severe spell of sickness this winter & was unable to go out of the house untill in the spring.

My father opened a large sugar orchard this spring and made a great quantity of sugar. Here he would leave me to attend the camp alone in the night.

When summer [1820] came I was again put to work in the corn field & other like agracultural pursuits, with about similar specimens of industry on my part as last summer. He [my father] raised also this season a large crop of excellent wheat.

This year a man named Joel Allen,[23] a distant relation of my fathers came into this settlement and put up at my uncle Isaac's, [and] commenced shoe-making for a livelihood, but in reality as a cover to his real character, for he had not been there long before he started to run away with one of my uncle's girls (Lydia)[24] & was overtaken by the old man and she was brought home and saved from infamy and ruin. for soon it was ascertained that [he] had been previously maried several times. He married several times near here & left his wives after living with them about seven or eight months.

This fall My-self and Allen had a hard spell of the Mumps. I in particular was very bad.

This winter I was sent to school to a man by the name of Hiram Madden;[25] but did not go long before a difficulty arose between me and some other schollars, and my father interfearing, caused a general disturbance, & I was taken away.

◆ A.D. 1821. ◆

This spring we moved about a half a mile south from where we now lived, to a place which my father had made some kind on contract to purchase, but never did. Here we raised another crop and also a very large crop of flax which yielded uncommonly well

This summer we recieved a letter from two of my sisters at Pleasant Hill Kentucky, desiring my father to come after them as they had left the Shakers.

He went after them; but before he got there; the shakers had induced them to come back. So he was disappointed and very much put out both with his daughters & the Shakers.

◆ A.D. 1822. ◆

My youngest sister (Elizabeth) was born this spring.[26] This was my mother's youngest child.

My father had made a bargain, and either rented or leased a place south from here, of a man named Adam Reynard[27] where he put in a crop.

Some time in the summer we receved another letter from my sister Mary desiring my father to come again and bring her home, as she had left the Shakers again. He went and found her living at one of his old friends Daniel Burfett's, who had allways been a good frend to my father.

While he was there preparing to start home my sister Anna left the shakers and came also. I had now left with the Shakers two more sisters, Rebeca & Margaret.

It was with great joy that my old mother saw two more of her daughters, who had been absent some seven years, but now restored to her embraces.

This winter Allen & my two youngest sisters, Lydia & Elizabeth, had the hooping cough which lasted all winter.

Some time this winter we received another letter from Kentucky from my sister Margaret, who had also left [the Shakers] and was at old friend Burfett

He [my father] went after her and took my sister Anna along, thinking perhaps she might induce Rebecca to come also But in this they were disappointed They however brought home Margaret some time in February 1823.—

◆ A.D. 1823. ◆

Earley this spring after returning from Kentucky my father bought in a large quantity of geese and undertook the business of "growing feathers" as the place on which we now lived had an abundance of grass and was well calculated to that business

But in the summer they became so anoying and troublesome to one of our neighbours (Grand-Dadda Simcock[28] as we called him) that he sold them off again before he effected much in the "feathered kingdom"

This summer my father raised a large crop on "Old Reynards place" again consisting principally of pumpkins, squashes, some corn and beans, melons and in the fall a large quant[it]y of turnips & parsnips.

This crop was raised on new ground which he had cleared the last year on a new contract which he had made to have the use of the land thus cleared for five years

Some time in the fore part of the summer or in the spring a man who called his name William Stout[29] a weaver by trade came into the settlement and became acquainted with my sister Margaret and obtained my fathers consent to marry her.

When the time drew near to be married he proposed to go to Lebanon as he had friends there to which my father objected, where upon they ran away, Mary going with them.

This put the old man out very much and he concluded to let them go but some of his friends pursuaided him to go after them.

Accordingly he started taking me along as I afterwards learned, to assist in killing "Bill" When we got there we found at the Clerks office that they were not married but getting on the track found them about dark about one mile from Lebanon.

He [William Stout] had gone to work at his trade with a good old long faced Du[t]ch Baptist and when he saw us was very much disconcerted and knew not what to say. My father abruptly demanded to know what he had done as he had for; but Bill could not say much.

The girls were now for the first time convinced that they had acted imprudently; and for the first time had to reflect that their exit from home was looked upon by the public as sencureable and their first impulse was never to return home again. But my father soon got them convinced of the best way to pursue & Mary agreed to return.

That night June the 6th, Bill was married to Margaret, which ended my father's jurisdiction over her. They had a good chance to make a living there by weaving so they staid and the next day we came home, with Mary along with us.

This was the first "Long journey" I had taken being 20 miles, to walk in a long dry summer day bare foot with only a shirt, hat & pantaloons on, my feet wore out on the gravel and I found it hard "sledding" Comming home however was not quite so hard, for about half way home and when very tired we came in company with a man who had two barrells of cider oil, very good.[30] He was drawing it to Wilmington to sell. When he started to travel it commenced to foment and he drew out some and put in water thinking to stop it, but it made it worse. This my father knew but said nothing. At length it became so bad that he commenced drawing it out and we all went to drinking at a round rate. This was fine times for me and made the road easy. It was the first I ever tasted & pleased me well Not knowing its power I drank deep, and long before I got home was under full sail beyond the bounds of cares and sorrow. Everything seemed to rejoice.

We came home thus in the evening of the 7th of June. None of the rest had partook so liberally as I, & were right side up when they came home, and of course I was the only one who could rejoice under the circumstances. So much for Bill.

I was taken down with, what was called the French measles, soon after our return from Lebanon.[31] Allen & my two youngest sisters also had the same complaint. We were very sick and for a while it was doubtful whether we would live or die; but we however all recovered.

We had but just recovered from the attact of the French measles before we were taken down with the spotted measles.[32] My father did not escape this time but came very near dying.

My youngest sister (Elizabeth) after partially recovering was taken down with a relapse and died. All the rest recovered after a very severe spell.

This fall my father sold out his claims on the "Reynard place" for some cattle & a rifle, to Reynard & he then commenced to butchering and selling beef at which he done well for a short time. This he had also done some summers previously with good success.

This summer my father took a notion to make his fortune by raising castor oil beans and had me and my brother [Allen] to plant large quantities of them both in and out of the fields and in the fall we geathered part of them & they spoilt on our hands and we never made anything by it.

Bill Stout came back this fall to see us and left Margaret at Lebanon He was here a day or two and would give us no satisfaction as to what he intended to do and so my father got in a rage at him and ordered him away, threatning to shoot him if he did not instantly g[o]. Bill however did not appear alarmed and said nothing It however proved only a "flare up" for the old man cooled off and done nothing & Bill went home and moved back in a short time & settled about four miles from here and went to weaving. His wife [Margaret] was very sick this fall and came home to live, but Bill never came in the house again, but went off some where, and was gone untill near spring His wife had agreed to leave him and go to Tennessee to her uncle Samuel Stout, my father's brother[33]

She accordingly started with a man & his wife, who was here by the name of Stanton. He lived near my uncle Samuel & was here on a visit to see his brother.

Bill came in the settlement soon after they left and started after them and overtook them and prevailed on her to live with him again.

This fall my mother was taken down with the consumption and before spring was confined to her bed.

This I believe closes the year as to anything of a characteristic nature, in the affairs of my fathers family.

◆ 1824 ◆

This spring my father put in a crop on the place where he lived & among other things put in a large quantity of cabbage which grew to an uncommon size. I worked with him untill about June and then hired to a man named Job Cooley, where I staid about a month and was employed at hoeing corn.

After this, I went to live with a man named Benjamin Howell,[34] who lived some more than a mile from home. When I went there to live, I felt as if I was seperated entirely from my little brother & sister who was very near to me, and for several days I thought of home & cried all the time that I was alone although I could run home any time in an hour; but it was the first time I was ever seperated from them for Cooley lived within a few hundred yards from my fathers I was engaged here at hoeing corn untill harvest and then put to harvesting. This was new work to me and went hard with me & I did not like it, but I was releived however from this for I got word from my mother that she was worse & wanted to see me. So I went home and staid a few days In the meintime [I] informed them how I was treated and my father would not let me go back but sent me back after my clothes. I went but did not tell that I was not coming to live with them any more but said I wanted to stay with my mother untill she got better for that was her request.

Howell was not at home but his wife gave me what clothes I took there and said that he had told her not to let me have any more I suppose they had expected that I would not come back to live. He had bought me some light, cheap summer clothers for "Sunday" amounting perhaps to one dollar and a half.

So he kept that and would allow me nothing for my work. He had treated me hard all the time I was with him and in fact he was mean, narrow contracted, and dishonest man & totally unfit to bring up a boy. I had to work very hard while there.

When I came home I found my mother much worse, for she was now very low, she continued to sink untill the 28th day of July when she died

By her death I lost the only unwavering friend that I had and our family was now left like a ship without a rudder to be the sport of misfortune and I severely felt and realized her loss, and now when deprived of her, could begin to see my own ingrattitude and disobedince to her, and when too late would gladly have served her.

The rest of the family now remained together a short time but did not go into any arraingements to live but all seemed lossed and knew not what to do, for our helm was gone.

The loss of my mother was a misfortune which reached my heart and caused me deep and lasting trouble, which I feel to this day when I ponder on her tenderness and goodness to me. Notwithstanding the lapse of twenty-three years between us and the many privations, misfortunes, losses in friends & perils which I have encountered since.

Not long after the death of my mother I went and worked for an old fat rich Quaker named John Fallis.[35]

Here I was put at making and mowing or packing away hay. He had a number of hands at work and I enjoyed myself well. I worked for 12½ cents a day untill I got cloth for a round about coat, and then went to live with his son-in-law Eli Harvey, who lived about 4 miles from there on the Lebanon road.[36] This seemed to me to be going to a strange and foreign land.

When I got there, I was struck with the familiarity of the place for as I came from Lebanon last year as mentioned before, well filled with cider oil, I had stopped to rest on the large projecting roots of a popler of uncommon size, about seven feet [in] diameter which from its singularity & size drew my attention & I had often thought of it It stood close to the road in an old "deadening" where I knew some body contemplated making a farm but appeared to me to be a "wildering maize" secluded from the haunts of man.

Here I found my new home and to me fell the task to convert this wilderness of dead timber into a fruitful field. Fallis took me down there & I went to work. There had been a small crop of corn put in last spring & a house built. Harvey was doing well.

My first work was to pick and burn brush. He was a pushing man in business and well calculated to learn a "spoilt child" to work I had to work hard earley and late I generally went home every Saturday to see my folks. He was the best man I ever lived with, good, kind, and obliging [He] would exact all that I could do and no more & was a good judge of the amount of work a boy should do. I soon found that he only wanted the fair thing and would not be satisfied without it He never misused, never repremanded or seemed to be dissatisfied with out I was to blame and I soon loved, obeyed, and respectd him and, what was still more strange I worked well and became interested in his welfare a thing before unknown to me.

Eli, was also a Quaker. This was the first summer that he had been married Here I enjoyed myself better than I ever had done before and felt that I was in a way to learn to be some account

Hitherto I did not think I was doing well and had nothing to encourage me, but now, full of hopes and bright expectations I assumed new life and determined to be worth something

I staid here till cold weather and went home again and again sank back into dispondency and gloom without anything before me to stimulate [me] to action

After remaining at home a while inactive, my father took a notion to take me to willmington to learn a trade.

He there put me to live with a man named Isaiah Morris,[37] who was clerk of the circuit court

Morris only wanted a boy to do his work, such as making fires taking care of the horses and such like drudgery and to this occupation I was doomed to serve for a season. He never allowed me to eat untill himself and all his family had done and then I came and "picked the bones" He was a very popular and influential man and was withal a good sort of a fellow, but too rich and consequential to stoop to tutor me more than to answer his purpose and further he cared not for my wellfare.

When I first came he gave me very positive orders not to be out after night as was the custom with other boys here, and that I had to be civil and industrous, which I thought at the time was perfectly right and intended strictly to observe it, for I had been thus far raised in a civil Quaker settlement and was in fact an uncommon civil boy, for the simple reason that I had never yet had the opportunity to learn anything else. The sequel will show how well I retained my loyalty and first love for I was not there many days before the Presidential election came off which resulted in the election of John Quincy Adams to the Presidency.[38] I was not allowed to go to see what was going on and be an eye witness to the election; but was engaged in burying cabbage close to the Court house and could hear the oaths and shouts for their respective candidates usual on such occasions all [of] which was so wild and uncivil to me that I did not know what to think for it was the first election I ever saw or even heard of.

The day passed off, and after dark the boys took the streets and commenced [shouting] mostly for Henry Clay, "Hurrah for Clay." "Hurrah for Adams, "Hurrah for Jackson" was ringing all over town. Some of Morris family wanted me to go and stop the boys, and accordingly I went, for I verily thought [this] was most ridiculous.

I did not lecture them long, for as soon as I came in company [with the boys], one of the boys told me to never mind but to Hurrah for Clay, which was no sooner said than I also took fire and commenced I believe louder than any one else. In a moment all my gravity was gone and I was the wildest one in the company. so unaccustomed was I to such freaks that once engaged [I] did not know how to govern myself, but [was] like a tame well diciplined young horse [which when] taken on supprise by a frightened wild drove is more impetu[ou]s than the rest, for I knew not what ailed me.

We continued thus along time when I sobered down and went home & very gravely complained at the reckless noisy boys who did not regard the good order of the place.

I was mightily taken up with the lively rude and good natured town boys at this time and thought them far preferable to my old civil Quaker comrades and was now anticipating great joy to be had in their society on "Sundays" when we could rove in innocent civil and friendly droves uninterupted by any thing to mar our good feeling and play; but in this I was doomed to be disappointed for the first Sunday when I met with a gang of them to "bask in plasure" they according to their custom had me to break as they called it for they alway made a country boy fight before they would acknowledge him as a regular playmate

This was something I was not prepared for and the last thing which I wished to do for I had the best of feelings for them all and only wanted innocent amusement.

Accordingly they commenced the opperation by aggravating me in every way that they could calling all manner of ill names and cursing me for a coward, while others were on my side & would tell me how to do and what was wanted and if I would whip any of the them all would be right, promising to see me have fair play Others told me how these same boys treated them when they first came in town to live.

There was one boy who I knew before he came to town for he had been one of our neighbours and he was now the foremost one to aggravate me His name was Elihu Millikin. Annother larger boy named Brooks Griffith told me that when he first came Elihu treated him as he was now me and that he took a long stick and began to poke his nose, saying that he would snuff the candle, and that he gave Elihu a good whipping and ever since Elihu had been a good friend to him and if I would only whip him that he knew Elihu would afterwards be a good friend to me and that I would be obliged to whip someone before I could have any peace with the boys Elihu heard all that was said and confirmed it but said I was such a coward that I darst not fight and swore that he would snuff my candle and so saying he took a long mullin stalk and commenced at my nose.

This began to put me in the proper mood for the case in hand.

Previously to this I had declared my unwillingness to fight and my feeling were so wounded at the ill treatment of the 6 boys that I wept with grief and disappointment

Elihu had not snuffed long at my nose before I told him what he might depend on in case he persisted but this only made him worse & he swore I darst not touch him.

About this time some of the boys gave me a push against him; at which he swore and threatned most bitterly while the boys repeatedly pushed me on him anxious to see a fight and I was now getting in the notion fast and when they pushed would yield to it a few times and at last, vexed all most to desperation I jumped at him and knocked him down and before he could recover, gave him three severe kicks in the small of the back which all most broke him down. He was in an instant scarcely able to walk and now cried and screamed most unmercifully for he was badly whiped. While I was at this the boys all shouted for me and unanimously hailed me as a first rate fellow except Elihu and he swore that he would yet have revenge, but I swore that if he attempted anything again I would whip him ten times worse for I was now ready for any kind of a fight and perfectly regardless of the consequences

Such was the manner of my initiation into manners and customs of the town boys.

Elihu, became a great friend of mine afterwards as the boys had told me but not steadfastly a friend untill I gave him three or four more severe whippings, after which he was always ready to take up on my side whether I was right or wrong

With all my civil Quaker habits and the disgust with which I first looked on the behavior of these boys I was soon one of the worst in town and in fact many became ashamed of me and often reproved me who I once thought so reckless and wild.

We would meet together late at night and wander in droves stoning houses and abusing the more civil part of [the] community and particularly if we had any thing against a man we were shore to do him a displeasure. This was the first winter I was there.

Such was a specimen of my life with the boys notwithstanding Morris' orders to the contrary.

I went home to see my people once and Allen came part of the way home with me, which was the last time I ever saw any of my people for years.

Not many weeks after this I came to see my people again full of joy and gratification with a light heart at the prospect of again being with my brother and sisters once more.

I came near the house and commenced making a noise to cause some of them to come out to see what was the matter, and then hid to disappoint them; but I soon found myself more sadly disapointed, for no one came out and wondering at the cause I went to the house and then found they had gone. The house was desolate. I knew in a moment that they had gone to Cincinnati for father had been making such calculations. I found myself in this lonely desolate place of my former joys, All gone far away & I here alone whereas I had anticipated so much satisfaction at this moment. But O, my people are gone It is impossible to describe my feelings. After looking around on the desolation which now brooded over everything in view I commenced weeping & most bitterly too. It seemed that I was the most forsaken being on earth and now doomed to eternal loneliness and sorrow & I must mourn out the remainder of my day. It seemed that I could heare the weak plantiff voice of my departed mother admonishing me to do better and would look in the house but alas she was gone & I truly alone and where is the family

Every object before me was a witness of better & happy day but all gone by all these things conspired to awaken my feelings and sorrow

It was now for the first time that my head pained me & seemed that my senses would leave with trouble I wept long and loud.[39]

At length I washed my face at a brook and dried up my tears and went to our nearest neighbor (Grandfather Simcock) to hear all that I could about the family.

I put on as a cheerful countenance as I could and went in. They confirmed my first idea that they had gone to Cincinnati and after staying there an hour or two I started home again, to Wilmington weeping and lamenting as I went & cast many a long lingering sorrowful look back to see my little brother I came to the place where he had accompanied me to when I saw him last and there seemed to part with him again.[40]

It is hard for a person to conceive the agony I was in when I came home and let Morris' folks know what had happened.

I served Morris purpose very well for a while but became dissatisfied for he did not treat me well.

He would not get me any new cloths for winter which I needed badly, but would have me wear some of his old one which made me look very odd for he was a large man. I knew I was not well treated and had no reason to expect anything for my advantage Neither good food clothing or any chan[c]e to go to school but saw I was only intended as a servant and I decreed in my heart to be of no use to him. This caused me to seek ways to shune work which thing I found I had quite a tallent and was soon able to make him earn all that I did before he could get me at it right. I would take care of the horses because I loved them and not for his sake.

During this winter I often heard from my father by the mail boys who went to Cincinnati twice a week (about 55 miles) which was some consolation to me even to hear from them and I expected that my father would come after me in the spring & I would go away, which kept up my spirits no little.

Thus passed this year as far as I can remember

◆ 1825 ◆

This year found me about as before described, and not much advantage to Mr. Morris, and looking for my father to come after me which kept me in great suspense for months and very uneasey. In the spring I was put to gardening. This occupation suited me very well had I been satisfied with my home and future prospects. In the summer I was most of my time rainging around town and through the surrounding country and up and down the creeks, with other like truants I evidently grew worse every day. Some times I would go alone to the destrict of my former days with my brother and rove through the woods whi[ch] we had been used to and give myself up to weeping & mourning in solitary loneliness

It was there I would resolve to amend my ways and do better for I knew I was going to ruin but had not government over myself to keep me strait when in town.

I would resolve to join the Methodist some times but did not know how neither had the moral courage [to] enquire. at other times I would resolve to leave town and go to a place better calculated to teach me better things but did not know how to leave Morris, because my father enjoined it on me to stay there and that seemed sacred to me now.

Amidst all these good and bad feelings I was tossed and would hardly get into town before all was over for the first boy I met I was as bad as ever notwithstanding my better desires when alone

Upon the whole in all my wild career, I was uncommonly wrought on about religion when my mind could be brought to reflection, and had any of the religious part of [the] community undertaken it would soon have brought me to the, "anxious seat" to get religion. but who would have thought so of me?

Some times I went to see my uncle Isaac's and my cousins. On one occasion I took Elihu along with me, while there I had a quarrel with a neighbor boy who was playing with us & my cousins, which gave them a full specimen of my "manner of speech" which perfectly astonished them for it was to them as rediculous as such things was to me when I first went to town

They informed my uncle of these things, who was not satisfied to see me let run thus uncontrolled and untaught, so he went and complained to Morris about it and wanted me to come away.

My uncle was a particular friend to Morris & he did not wish to do anything to displease him and so he agreed to do as he [my Uncle Isaac Stout] desired. Thus by doing evil, good came for my outragious bad language & habits served to awaken my uncle to a sense of duty and thus delivered me from such a place which nothing else could for Eli Harvey had been to see me to go and live with him again a thing most desireable to me, but Morris objected & I undertook to run away which he found out and pursuaded me not to do notwithstanding he so readily yielded to my uncle.

Accordingly in December I left him and went and lived with my cousin Jesse Stout. where I staid till the end of the year

Here I was at once delivered from all bad company at which I felt happy & had the society of my cousins to play with.

Jesse was a very civil Quaker but would chop fire wood on the Sabbath. This I thought most sacralagious, for it was not alowed in town & I was consciencious about it as bad as I was & thought I would prepare wood for him the day before. Such a mixture of religion and devilment.

◆ 1826 ◆

This year found me with Jesse Stout. I cut my foot in the later part of winter which disabled my from work and I went to stay with my uncle While here doing nothing I took a notion to learn to wright, so my cousin Isaac, who was about my age undertook to learn me. He wrote a good hand. Suffice it to say it was not long before I wrote a tolerably legible hand. When I was able to work I went to Jesse's again and he set me to studdying arithmetic at which I soon learnt the first rules This was a great start to me in education and gave me such a taste for it that I could not be satisfied Had Morris taken any pains with me I now could have been a tolerable good schollar. I resolved now to have an education and to that end all my thought and intentions were bent

Some time in April Eli Harvey, learning where I was, came to see me and wanted me to live with him again which I was glad to do & it also suited Jessee very well for he did not need me & accordingly went immediately home with him

I now felt perfectly restored and redeemed from all trouble for I had often thought and sighed for the privilege of again living with him. I was here put to regular work again for the first time since I left him & rejoiced at the privilege but found I had contracted indolent habits which however he was well calculated to cure without any harsh words or bad feelings.

I commenced by preparing the ground for a crop, by burning up the logs & limbs which had fallen in the winter.

When the time came I was put to ploughing. This suited me well. I was delighted with a farmers occupation and can say that I worked hard this summer.

It was a Quaker custom to go to meeting twice a week and this privilege was granted to me and [I] mostly went and civilly and willingly conformed to all the sober habits of a Quaker life and took a great interest in Harvey's wellfare. All the boys in the neighborhood were civil Quakers & I could have no bad company had I desired it. I felt like I was doing some good for mys[e]lf and hopes began to arise again This summer was spent in all the common occupations of farming and clearing ground at such times as we were not needed on the farm.

I was also very attentive to my book and improved every leisure moment I had and was always assisted by Eli when needed in anythings I could not understand, for he was a good school master, and ready to teach which was a great benefit to me.

I will mention a word about Quaker meetings. When you go to a quaker meeting you will sit with your hat on & nothing said, that is all sit with hats on no one speaks unless the spirit moves him to. Meeting lasts generally about one hour. They "break" or dismiss meeting by the head ones Shaking hands and then all arise and go out.—

This winter Eli took up a school about one & half miles from his house and I went to school to him for a term of three months.

I made great proficiency in my studdies this winter. Besides improving my hand writing considerable I went about one third through the arithmetic. I gave close attention to study and would not allow myself time to play but seldom.

I was well done by this year by Eli for besides sending me to school three month and my victuals and clothes he gave me a new suit of cloths which was entirely ahead of anything I had ever had before and [I] now made a fine tall appearance & I then thought very grand.

This closes the history of this year.

## ◆ 1827 ◆

This spring I commenced work; after school was out, with Eli, on new terms. Instead of working for my vuictals and clothes as usual, Eli thought I ought to have something more, so he proposed giving me three dollars pr month for five months, besides doing my washing mending, and making my clothes. I was to "take the weather as it comes" as the saying then was that is counting wet and dry. This was his own arraingement and I agreed to it not doubting his judgement which was however for those times about right He also used to give me extra jobs and pay me for it which considerably increased my wages.

I worked out the five months without loosing a single day for if I was sick he always lost the time and not me.

I worked as before at farming. At the end of the five months he was eight dollars in my debt for which he gave me his note five of which was to be in cash and the residue in cloth. This was also his own contract.

After I was done work here I worked at several different places as I met with chances, mostly for eighteen cents pr day and also was back and forth to my uncle Isaac's several times, but my home [was] at Eli's.

In the fall Eli paid me the five dollars in money which was the first time I ever had more than a dollar at once & I now thought of laying it up to buy land as soon as I could get enough.

I went to Willmington this summer a time or two, & there saw my old town mates but had no disposition to live there nor did I like their company, for I was now fairly a Quaker in my heart and intended some day, when I learnt how, to join their society. I was in fact a truly religious boy but no one knew or even supposed that I had any such feelings.

Thus passed off this summer and fall and in the winter Eli Harvey took up another school where he did last year & I went and lived with David Harvey his brother & went to school to Eli I worked evenings & mornings for my board and was to work one week for him after school was out.

I was very attentive to my studies this winter and made about the same proficiency as I did last winter and went about two thirds through the arithmetic. I seldom went to play at noon.

This winter I had an affair with one of the school boys which I believe taught me the first lessen I ever received on human nature.

There was a boy named Samuel Savage who was not a Quaker. He was a most profane and quarelsome fellow and all the boys and girls at school hated him. He was alway disputing at play time and threatning to fight while he well knew the Quaker boys would not; but I often heard them wish some one would whip him.

At length he commenced abusing me. A thing I would by no means bear so I told him one day in great earnest that I would whip him if he did not behave which only made him worse, for he did not believe me and accordingly the next day he brought a number of small stones in his pocket and showed them to me in time of school and was making his brags all the forenoon how he would use them on me if I attempted to hurt him. All the boys and girls expressed their disapprobation at his conduct and unanimously declared that he ought to be whiped

I knew I had the decision of the whole school on my side and verily thought it would be a righteous act to whip him and also a great accommodation to all the schollars accordingly at play time I went out with the rest to play ball & he was very crabbid and swore if I hit him with the ball even when it was in order that he would hit me with a stone so the first chan[c]e for a throw I got I aimed at him while he squared himself to throw back; But I was at him before he had time to throw back and while he was taking the stone out of his pocket [I] jumped on him and gave him a most unmerciful beating over the head with my fist which almost entirely disabled me from writing for a day or so.

Eli soon came out and gave me a severe repremand for my "Town boy capers" and threatened to dismiss me from school. The schollars unanimously turned against me and simpathized for Samuel Savage calling me fighter. I now found I had done a thankless job for it was as much to accommodate them as to gratify my own feelings. The fact was they did not really want any one whiped and while saying so did not expect to see it done. Whereas I was in earnest and thought they were also.

This was heralded all over the settlement to my disadvantage but I stood up for myself.

I learned that it was not good policy to do fighting for people who had not corurage or a disposition to do it for themselves and it proved a useful lessen to me in after life and caused me to begin to observe the inconstancy and ingratitude of mankind & no doubt it has prevented me from falling into worse difficulties by trying to help those who will not help themselves For if you ever do you may depend on being forsaken in times of trouble.

My sister Mary, who moved to Cincinnatti with my father in the fall of 1824, had been married to a man named [Nicholas] Jameson at or near a place then called the 18 mile Island below Louisvill I believe on the Ohio river

She was married January 7th 1825 She had one son called Benjamin Walter Jameson, who was born December 3rd 1825 and died October the 3rd 1826.

My father had moved from Cincinnati down the river stopping at several places for a short time untill he came to the above named point where Mary was married from whence he proceeded on as will be related hereafter, scattering his family by the way.

This fall My Uncle Isaac received a letter from Jameson which informed us that Ma[r]y was dead. She died January the 5th 1827, of consumption, I think.

During the term of the above named school I went to my uncles on a visit, as was always my custom occasionally when I was informed of the death of Mary & the situation of my peple there.

This news was communicated to me immediately upon my coming into the hous, which perfectly shocked me and filled me with grief & sorrow which I could only give vent to in a flood of tears.

There is a possibility of me being mistaken in the time I received the above news It might have been last winter.

◆ 1828 ◆

This Spring when the school was out I was almost entirely destitute for clothes for such had been my eagerness for schooling that I would not stop untill the expiration of the term and on the last day of the school I was litterally flying in rags with both knees out bare and had not went to meeting or any pub[l]ic place except school for a long time.

After the school was out I commenced work again with double dilligence, determined now to fit myself out again with respectable clothing, accordingly I commenced work again for Eli Harvey first for twenty-five cents a day. I then went to work for a man named Ezekiel Hornaday[41] for four dollars pr month at preparing and putting in spring crops. I believe I worked for him two months and then Jesse Harvey a Doctor and cousin to Eli came and offered me five dollars a month to work for him. To which propersition I accepted and quit Ezikiel to his great disappointment and chagrin for Jesse had fairley over bid and underminded him. but I Did not think anything about [this] at the time but the first chance Eli Harvey got he told me that Jessee had no right to interfere without first going to see Ezekiel & having an understanding with him. I then thought so too but it was now too late for I had bargained with Jessee and went accordingly.

He [Jesse Harvey] set me to clearing ground and rolling logs alone and of course I done but little.

Sometimes he would come out and work and tear about a while fresh from his apothecary shop and then hint to me that I ourght to work accordingly.

After a while he set me to ploughing with a weak starved poor team and a bad plough on the new rooty ground at which I made poor headway.

His horses were fed on a scant portion of bran and were in fact unable to work.

He had likewise some old ground to plough at which I done very well at for a while.

He never had enough cooked to eat and this had always been said of him that he starved his hands.

In fact he was a mean narrow contracted little soured man, having but last winter finished his studdies at Cincinnatti & now had this spring set up for business, deeply in debt, and had no practice worth naming. He sat in his house and spent his time in reading and his studdies and at the same time was unable to support his family, which was large He had evidently undertook to cut a big figure before he was properly qualified for it He was not very po[p]ular. He was ready to grind down a hired boy like me for a trifle.

The result was, I soon became dissatisfied and tried as little to please him as he did to do justice by me and we fell out before harvest and parted.

On settlement he refused to pay me all my dues and acted most rascally and mean with me.

After leaving him I worked but little more in that settlement but while there made my home at Eli's.

During the time of Harvest I went from this settlement to my uncles again and there commenced going to school to George Carter who had taught school at a school house near Lytle's creek meetinghous, almost time out of mind, for all that now lived in the vicinity had been educated by him who were under middle age.[42] He had educated all my uncle's family many of whom were now married & many of his former pupils were now sending their children to him also.

He was a good schollar and teacher. I boarded at my uncles & went to school to him & commenced the studdy of English Grammar by Saml Kirkham[43] at which I had allready quite a smattering. I went about six weeks to him during which time I applied myself closely to my studdys & acquired a tolerable good knowledge of grammar. I also assisted my uncle to do his harvesting.

While here going to school one of my second cousins Stephen Stout[44] came and wanted me to go to the Illinois with him as he was going to move this fall to which I agreed in case he could take also my sister. Peggy [Margaret] also which he did for it all suited him very well and accordingly I now began to arrainge my business for it.

My sister Margaret had as before mentioned started to Tennessee to my uncle Samuel Stouts with Staunton, but her husband [William Stout] overtook them and she was again induced to live with him and not go to my uncles so they were together a short time & he again left her somewhere in Kentucky, in a most desolate condition shortly after which she was del[i]vered of a son [Samuel] October the 8th 1824 who died Nov. 1826. Being left in her delicate situation in a strange land poor and destitute she suffered incredibly but at length obtained news somehow or other of Jameson & her twin sister Mary his [Jameson's] wife contrived means [for Margaret] to come to her.

When she came she was sick and scarcely able to walk & So was Mary also sick

Their meeting can better be imagined than described for Mary was not apprized of her coming untill she saw her at her door & both wept unable to speak for a while. She [Margaret] remained with Mary untill her death and in the spring of the present year came here again and had remained here untill the time now mentioned.

I wound up my schooling sold off my desk & things that I could not move & then went to Todd's Fork[45] again to settle up some out standing accounts I had there. While there Eli Harvey wanted to know what I was going to do. I told him I was going to Mackinaw.[46]

This he did not like, for upon some others coming up and making similar inquiries Eli told them that I was going to the lead mines[47] where it was no harm to swear.

He thought that the Mackinaw country [Illinois] & lead mines was all one and such was the universal idea although it was 180 miles to the lead mines from Mackinaw.

The fame of the profanity of the lead mines was proverbial & Eli thought it would be my ruin to go there.

I wound up my business there and bid them all farewell for the last time and have never saw them since.

Shortly after this my sister Margaret & myself went home with Stephen stout to prepare for our intended journey.

He lived on Grassy Run about 12 miles from my uncles & beyond willmington that is North East.[48]

This [the place where cousin Stephen Stout lived] was a level flat wet country and very uninviting being the heads of the Todd's Fork & Lytle creeks and some others. I here had several cousins and formed a fast and quick acquaintance with many.

I here first began to keep company with the girls and now began to wish I was married

I staid here some two or three weeks while stephen was preparing to move & we then moved down on Todds Fork near Centre Meeting house where his father lived and there prepared for his final start.

While here I returned to my uncles [Isaac Stout's] to bid them all farewell and staid all night and the next day went back when nothing now remained but to go but before I start I will say a word about my father.

He had returned here about one year ago and had been living mostly by himself during the time & I had been to see him several times and staid all night He came by Jamesons on his way here & had brought back my little Sister Lydia so that now there was five of the family in the settle[ment] of Lytles creek namely Lydia Margaret, Sarah, myself & my father.

Anna & Allen were now in Illinois near where I was going

So you see we were now going to have another separation for none but myself & Margaret were going. My father had bound my sister Lydia to Adam Reynard a distant relation so I did not expect to see them again for years.

After returning from my uncles I believe we started the next day (Sept 9th) leaving my cousins with tears in our eyes, and pursuid our journey West.

We [Hosea, Margaret, and Stephen Stout] traveled through Waynesville Dayton &c Ohio to Richmond and along the National road[49] to Indianapolis, Indiana. Allmost all the road from Richmond to Indiana was uncommonly bad. The land was a flat level Beech land thick set with spice wood.[50]

The National road was now being cut out, which had been let out in different jobs & was now full of logs and trees felled across the road and lay there while we had to zigzag from side to side of the road across the State through a disagreeable mud all the way

I drove Stephens cattle and came on foot all the way.

I believe we were sixteen days journeying.

After crossing the Wabash river we soon came to the grand prairie which I had heard so much talk about and it was truly a grand scenery to me for I gazed upon the boundless ocean of meadow before me, which seemed to meet the horrizon on all sides except an ocasional grove which presented a dark line in the distance, with unmingled delight.

It was the first time that my eyes ever beheld such a wide expanse. Just before me I thought I beheld a beautiful elevation some twenty feet high like a wave & to that I pushed forward to have a more wide and extended view from its sumit of the wide spred prairie but I traveled hard for [a] long time still looking forward to the high grounds before me untill weary and fatigued I looked back & saw another elevation behind me which explained the matter for I did not know how to look upon a prairie & my eyes had decieved me for the country was a beautiful level.

I gazed with admiration and delight upon the beautiful scenery before me as I journeyed along, untill my eyes pained me and my head ached which was in consequence of not being accustomed to such an extended view, I suppose.

It was in the afternoon, & over a level dry prairie before I came to any timber or found watter.

This was my initiation into a prairie life in recieving which I partook of both the good & the bad in a measure, for I was allmost suffocated with heat and drouth when I got through and eagerly plunged into the first brook I came to, with the cattle & all drank together of a putrid stagnant stream & better watter I thought I never drank, but not with standing all this I was highly pleased with a prairie country from that day forth until now.

Suffice it to say our journey was now through prairie all the way passing through groves like islands in the midst of the ocean

It was a rich & beautiful country through which we passed and [was] now under a rapid state of improvement and cultivation. This was about the 20th day of september, when I first came into the prairie.

We arrived at the end of our journey about the 25th of September where we found my uncle Ephraim[51] and all his family. Jesse Stout, son of my uncle Isaac and some more, settled in a grove called Stout's Grove, from my uncle Ephraim who was the first settler in the grove although there was now a number of inhabitants in it many of whom had good farms, now open & some was just beginning.[52]

But the whole county around was new notwithstanding all the groves had now more or less inhabitants in them.

Stout's Grove was a most beautiful and delightful place, with good timber and prairie well calculated for farming.

It was from one to four miles wide & five or six long and lay about six or seven miles East of Mackinaw town the county seat of Tazewell County in which the grove lay.

From the most elevated parts of the prairie near this grove you have an extended view of the wide spread prairies before you bespotted with beautiful groves of timber so well calculated to captivate the feelings of a new comer & I was truly captivated, and am to this day with that country.

I remained a few days here during which time I visited all my relations in the grove, and rested from my journey, for I was almost given out with sore feet from hard walking and fatigue. after which I proposed going to where my brother & sister Allen & Anna was, a distance of about 20 miles West.

I started on foot and went to a grove about seven miles off on a stream called little Mackinaw Here my uncle Samuel Stout and the most of his children lived. They had lately came from Tennessee. I went to my uncles & he not being at home, made myself know to the family, all who seemed glad to see me.

After staying an hour or so and taking dinner I proceeded on passing by some of my cousins, to whom I also introduced myself and was well recieved, from there I proceeded to Samuel Whiten a cousin, and staid all night & in the morning procured a horse of him belonging to Amasa Stout[53] in Stouts Grove, and started to Dillen's Settlement.[54] So called where Anna & Allen lived.

I undertook to take a near rout to the settlement through the woods and got lost amidst the hill in an oak woods called "barrens"[55] Here I wandered untill noon and at length found myself to the East of Little Mackinaw grove and finding another new cousin, whom I had not before seen (John Stout, called Big John)[56] [I] got directions how to cross the Mackinaw river and go to the place I intended & so I proceeded onwards and in the evening found Anna & Allen.

Anna was living at Daniel Hodson's[57] formerly of Ohio Clinton County, & Allen with Martin Myers Son-in-law to Hodson.

Anna knew me on sight but Allen had lost all knowledge of my looks & knew me not.

They were doing well and was exceedingly rejoiced to see me.

I came here in a worn out situation for I had had a hard days ride in my wanderings having no saddle.

I here rested myself and some more and in a day or two I set out for Stout's Grove again accompanied by my Sister Anna. We set out on horseback I still had no saddle which made my ride anything but pleasant and agreeable.

We returned home by way of Mackinaw town. I was taken sick on the way and had to lay down several times before I got to town in the prairie for I was very stupid & sleepy and would fall to sleep almost as soon as I was down. Had not Anna been along to wake me up no doubt but I should have lain there till dark for I was very sick, weak & stupid. However we made out to get to Mackinaw town in the afternoon & put up at a public house, which was in fact all the house then occupied in the place. There was some more houses however but no ground improved. The city was thick set with oak shrubs & hazel and all the small shrubry common to the barrens also some scattering oak trees. It looked but little like a town & county seat It lay about one mile East of the Mackinaw river and if improved would be a handsom town. There was no store or grocery

The house was kept by Mr. Jonas Hittle,[58] a clever, fine man

We were well received by his wife who went to preparing our dinner; but I could not set up and called for a bed and laid down.

When dinner was prepared I was unable to eat and had all the symtoms of an approaching spell of sickness and so Anna eat her dinner and went on to Stout's Grove, being very anxious to see Margaret, and left me at Hittle's, where I was kindly treated by his wife for several days during which time I was very sick Mrs. Hittle was kind and attentive to me while here & I wanted for nothing.

As soon as I was able to go I was sent for and took up to the grove and in a few days was able to go around. My sickness came on by hard travelling on the journey & exposure on the road.

I was not here long before I began to think about going to work. Before I go [telling of my going] to work however I will inform you of another circumstance.

Amasa Stout a cousin was to be married in a short time after I came there. He lived at my uncle Ephraims [and] had been with him for the last ten years There were great preparations being made for the wedding & invitations were given to allmost to all the surrounding country.

The day came at length for the wedding. The party had mostly convened at the girls mothers about 4 miles below my uncles, towards Mackinaw town

I was yet very weak & feeble & did not go down; but waited till they came along.

They came forming a long procession by two's on horseback when I & my sister anna joined them. Margaret not being able to go.

We had now to go about six miles to Brown's grove[59] to the residence of "Preacher" Brown who was to solemnize the nuptials.

We had a pleasant ride, each one selecting the girl that suited him best and rode with her if he could get the chan[c]e Some however got "cut out" on the way

The Parson & family were all ready for us, together with a large company met on the occasion. Bars & gates were opened for us when we came

The procession marched three times around his house and then all dismounted and went in. I was introduced to the Parson who gave me his hand for better acquaintance as he said for he knew my father in Tennessee.

We had not been there long before, the parties were lawfully married and seated when all hands went in succession to wish them much joy, shaking hands & the men kissing the bride I did not partake in this for I did not know what it meant for it was the first time ever I saw any one married only in the Quaker way.

My uncle David Stout lived in this [Brown's] grove. He had a large family & some of his boys and girls were along with us.

After we were through here we all returned to the Brides mother's, (widow Smith) where we spent the night in plays, songs chat & sparking according to the New country customs which was entirely new to me, but easy to learn. I joined in all these amusements and enjoyed myself uncommonly well

We spent the whole night.

I in the morning we all went to uncle Ephraims to the "Infair"[60] where we were recieved well. Uncle took up a large quantity of honey of which he had an abundance and here we feasted and enjoyed ourselves uncommonly well untill we all were willing to go home. So much for the new country wedding.

I was much pleased with the appearance of this company, which was so different from any I had ever before witnessed and yet [was] so easy, familiar, and accessible in their manners.

They were dressed in plain clothes the young men had every variety of "home made" common blue & different home died bark coulered jeans, very ordinary hats & in fact every thing made in keeping with the kind of clothes

The girls dressed in common calico but few had any thing but calico bonnetts & all made simple & plain all perfectly harmonized with the Quaker teachings of plainess which I had allwa[y]s heard but never saw acted out before.

Some how or other I felt perfectly at home with them although in ohio I considered my best to be but ordinary yet on this occasion I entirely out shined them all, & eagerly drank in the customs of the county, captivated as much at their rustic manners as at the beautiful new country. All these things together made me unusually well contented & I according wrote to ohio to inform my relations there how well I was suited.

After the wedding & I had recovered my strength my cousin Ephraim proposed hiring me a month and offered me ten dollars this seemed a most exhorbitant price for five in ohio was the most I had ever got & the best hands there got but eight.

It was allmost as much as my conscience would allow to take notwithstanding it was the current wages. I was here accounted a full hand.

I finished this month for my cousin & set in for another at eight dollars as it was now in the winter. We was employed at gathering corn mostly.

Business was carried on here very differently from any way I had been accustomed to in ohio for instead of being up and out at work at daylight driving and pushing everything we never went to work untill after late breakfast and then no hurry and would stop along time before night.

I felt restless at this way of doing business which seemed so verry slow, after working with Harvey as long as I had. I was in a hurry but all was satisfied & would pay me for my time and have it idled away thus.

This winter Margaret was taken with the consumption & her and Anna went to Dillon's Settlement to have her attended by Dr. Griffith[61] a celebrated phisician who lived there. They staid there a while and returned back, bringing Allen along with them and he made cousin Ephraims his home and Margaret & Anna made their home at Uncle Ephraims while I was at work as above, alternately for both my uncle [Ephraim] & cousin [Ephraim, Jr.] as it suited my convenience

This was our situation about mid winter. I had in this grove [Stout's], Brown's Grove & Little Mackinaw [Grove] Three Uncles' and about 70 cousins and my old Grandmother Stout now upwards of 90 years old She was not able to walk & was very childish she was very glad to see us and called us Jo's children. She was constantly attended by an old maiden aunt her daughter Margaret Stout who was over 70 years I had likewise another aunt on Little Mackinaw.[62]

Jesse Stout took up a school late this winter to which I went a short time and improved in the arithmetic and writing, considerably.[63]

His school lasted untill time to stop for spring crops.

### ◆ 1829 ◆

This year found me going to school.

Margaret had been wearing out with the consuption all winter nor did any medical aid do her any good, as all fall under the with[er]ing touch of the consumption, so she fell. She died on the 28th day February and was buried in the buring ground in this grove [Stout's Grove], where as yet there had been but few cases.

I worked awhile for Jessee Stout this spring and then went to work for Mr. James Watson, a brother-in-law to my uncle Ephraim, to fill a prior engagement which I had previously made with him, in the winter to pay for a colt I had purchased of him for 35 dollars in work & had made a turn of 8 dollars to my uncle in the winter & now was to pay the rest in holding the prairie plow at 50 cents pr. day. However I had made 2,000 rails for him previously that is hired most of it done.

I worked along time for him and soon had my colt paid for. This was the first personal property I ever owned. Watson was a good man to work for I like to be with him but more of him hereafter.

The past winter some time my relations, all of whom believed in the Quaker tenets of religion who had any real belief at all, That is those in Stouts Grove, took a notion to hold Quaker meetings every sunday at Cousin Ephraim's and according they all would congregate on that day these accompanied by some more who was there who believed in the same faith.

It was the request of the most faithful among them that I should attend punctually as my influence would induce the rest of the youngsters to attend. which thing I consented to for I was yet as Quakerish as ever in my feelings.

We had several old fashioned Quaker meetings when the fame & the novelty thereof began to spread and attract the attention of the other young people and they altogether out of curiosity began to attend also not behaving any too well for they would wink & laugh at each other and inquire if the spirit moved them during meeting This I did not like for some of them were professors of religion and it gave me a very poor opinion of them.

This was the first religious persecution.

The inhabitants of this grove were all friendly and united untill now and after this religious move of the Quakers they manifested a narrow, bigoted feeling towards all the rest, and deprecated all who went to their meetings, which broke out in "open hostilities by & by.[64]

In the spring the Methodists & Cumberland Presbyterians[65] some of each living in the grove, began to hold meetings & Anna who was a methodist would go, which soon started me & Allen I had no religious motive in going what ever. But when I would go my uncle & cousin Ephraim would show great dissatisfaction & chagrin, throwing out insulting & slanderous insinuations & sometimes lies about them [the Methodists], which soon set me to defending them, when It was not long before cousin Ephraim informed me that if I went to any but Quaker meetings I could not come to his house notwithstanding he was still my friend and if I should be taken sick he would be ever as ready to take me in and administer to me as ever he was.

This information of Ephraim did not have much impression on me at first, but when I came to think upon it and found he had prescribed me in my religious opinions & was ready to turn me out of his house in case I did not hold to Quakerism, I began to despise him in my heart for as yet there had been no impression made on my mind religiously & I felt as well towards their Quaker meetings as ever & was just as willing to attend them notwithstanding I was going to the other meetings and gliding along with the tide of the young people, without having the subject of religion ever spoken of among us. He [Cousin Ephraim] was afraid I would lead his brothers and sisters off from Quakerism and took this method to separate us, for he said my Uncle [Ephraim] was of his opinion about me going to his house

This was the beginning of a prejudice between us which never has as yet been overcome.

I was living with James Watson at this time, and soon after I informed him of the conditions which I had to keep the friendship of my uncle & cousin upon and he spoke very positively against any such a bigoted set of religionests and advise me to simply keep away according to their request for there was more respectable people & more liberal minded in the grove than they, and I thought so too, but said nothing about it, and here the matter ended for the present.

There had been a debating school got up in the winter which was composed of all parties at first I was appointed Clerk as I was altogether the best schollar in the grove. This did not continue long before religious bigotry began to show itself through in many places and the school ran out in the spring and died a natural death.

Divisions now began to spread more and more untill in the summer or rather in the spring [1829] a Mr. Archibald Johnson took up a school for a term of one year.[66] None of my relations or any of the Quaker party would send to him or have anything to do with it but got up a school of their own in opposition. This was called the Quaker school.

During this time I was living with Watson and working to pay for my colt which I bought last winter of him, and now did not often go among my relations.

Mr. Johnson was a young man of very ordinary talents and not a very good schollar but done well enough to teach a school here. He was a Cumberlan[d] Presbeterian exhorter, a very poor speaker withall & very narrow contracted & bigoted in his feelings but very zealous & would hold meetings & preach every sunday in the different groves & some times here [in Stout's Grove]. Notwithstanding he was a clever honest & inoffensive man & I liked him tolerably well. He was too lazy to enjoy good health & would lay in bed till school time in the summer which made him look sickly & pale.

About this time I had a falling out with cousin Ephraim and took Allen away from his house and he also came to Mr. Watsons and lived.

Anna had also went away from our relations and was now living with Mathew Robb Esqr. We were now entirely on the anti Quaker party

After we were done breaking prairie & the hurry of spring work was over I commenced going to school to Mr. Johnson and boarded at Watsons at 50 cents a week or a days work. Allen was also sent to school with me by Watson.

I suppose I went about three months to school and here improved some little, my handwriting went through Kirkhams Grammar & also studdied arithmetic. Johnson was no very good schollar & when I left of[f] going to him was as good a schollar as he was.

I enjoyed myself well while going to school for I was suited well with my home and school mates, many of whom were about my age [nineteen] and we there formed ties of friendship which never has been severed.

My uncle Ephraim, who was a wise & cunning old smooth toungued "Snake in the grass" took great umbrage at us all and to revenge himself somewhat, he being one of the County commissioners, reported Allen as an orphan without a home and applied to the Commissioners Court to have a Guardian appointed so as to have him bound out as this would put him entirely out of my control for he was not willing for him to stay at Watson purely out of spite to us.

When I learned this my wrath almost arose beyond endurance however no accident happened & so when I learned the law on the subject I made an agreement with Mr. Watson, who was willing to have Allen bound to him and then we went to the man who had been appointed his [Allen's] guardian & had him bound to Watson. Thus we thwarted my uncle's plans, for he intended to have him away from there. We were now all well satisfied now and here it rested for the present.

From this time forth I detested both my uncle & cousin Ephraim for they were doing all that they could to breaks us down, but all the rest of the grove was on our side & we stood high in their estimation & had more friends than they.

Some more of my cousins sided with them but still was friendly to us Uncles David & Samuel did not participate in this crusade against us neither did they say or do any thing in our favor but remained nutral & friendly to both & I never had any bad feelings towards them, notwithstanding I seldom now ever went among any of them.

While I was going to school there was to be a camp meeting in Dillens settlement to which I & some more of my school mates went named Berry who professed to be religious. Anna was at this time there We went and I was introduced to the Preachers, all of whom seemed to take great notice of me and were very friendly & I was now in the midst of the holy Methodist religion and bouyed along on the tide I knew not how but I attended very strictly to preaching and was wonderfully wrought up and went forward to the anxious seat to be prayed for & here I struggled & prayed and contended for religion, a change of heart, to pass from death unto life &c &c. during the whole camp meeting at the proper times, exceedingly sober and surley tried to the best of "my skill and ability" but did not effect anything. Did not realize what I had heard described so often by them & towards the last of the meeting when oppertunity was given I & all my school mates joined the Methodists on trial for six month as was their custom. The young Berrys were Cumberlands before and now came over to the Methodists Thus ended the meeting & I came home under "contrivance of mind"

When I came home I still went to school & found that my literary desires were not overcome in the least by my religious ones for I made as great proficiency as ever. Joining the Methodist gave my uncle & cousin great scope to talk about me now and they did so

I was very punctual to attend meetings now & after this we had regular preaching every week. & not long after a two days meeting thinking to spread the Holy fire a little more in this grove but in this they failed for no more joined.

Matters rested thus for a time.

Some time in the latter part of the season my father came from Ohio, bringing, Sarah & Lydia along with him He had managed to get Lydia away from Adam Reynard, to whom she was bound when I left, which thing he done by common consent of the parties Our whole family was now together who were now living consisting of six persons in all [Joseph; sons Hosea and Joseph Allen; daughters Anna, Lydia, and Sarah]. My father had got religion in Ohio & said he was glad to see me also inclined religiously.

He was not here long before he began to interfere with the case of Allen's being bound, which caused him to have a terrible falling out with uncle Ephraim about which much was said. Allen and myself still at Mr. Watsons all this while. He [my father] fell out with almost all his brothers before he was here long & so he took a course to suit himself & before spring managed to have the indentures taken and Allen released & took him with him and went to live at Little Mackinaw. Sarah & Lydia was along also but I still remained at Watsons.

This fall [1829] I went to Funk's grove[67] about 12 miles south and worked awhile & cutting up corn for which I could get cash and then returned to Watson where I staid all winter

Our religion still went on & I attended a camp meeting in the Blooming grove[68] as a regular Methodist

We had also one in Stouts grove at all of these I was very zealous but still could not get the power Mr. Watson got religion at a camp meeting also and we had great times Watson joined the Cumberland & I soon discovered a hostile spirit between them and the Methodist which I thought very uncalled for It threw me much in the back grounds to hear preachers slander each other because of small different of opinion in "nonessentials" so called.

### ♦ 1830 ♦

I was quite religious this spring I worked some for Mr. Watson earley in the spring and then went down to Dillin's settlement to hire out in order to get me some clothes as I was now needy, but did not meet with an opportunity and came back to Stouts Grove and staid untill some time in the summer and again set out and went by there again to Pekin,[69] a town on the Illinois river, and there found an oppertunity to get work about 15 miles up the river on Ten mile creek where there was a mill in progress of building So I started in the afternoon to that place; but missed my road and got lost and wandered about untill near dark when I came to a man plowing in a field & I went to him to enquire the road & found that I had wandered some four or five miles out of the way.

I staid all night here.

The man's name was Morris Phelps,[70] who, on finding out my business, proposed hiring me in case I did not suit myself at the place I was going to.

The next morning I went on & arrived at the Ten Mile [Creek] at noon and went to work and only worked one day not liking neither the place, the kind of work, nor any of the men but felt myself in perfect confinement so the next day after dinner, taking an order on a store in Pekin for 50 cents for my days work I set out on the back track & came to Mr. Phelp's again and made a bargain with him to work at ten dollars a month.

The next morning I went to Pekin and took up my order & then returned to Dillen's Settlement to Mr. Hodson's where my sister Anna now lived and made arraingements to go to work for Mr. Phelps. I worked at Mr Phelp's two months. He was a tolerably good man to work for notwithstanding he oppressed me considerable in my wages on settlement and was very austeer and grouty at times. However I liked him on the main very well His wife was a fine clever woman and was very kind and good to me. He lived three miles from Peoria on the road leading from thence, through Dillon's settlement to Springfield at a place called the "Willow Springs"

I was employed at farming rail making, and some times at work at a mill which he & some more were building on Farm creek.[71] I enjoyed myself very well while here. Phelps was a Methodist back slider & his wife s[t]ill good in the faith which was company for me.

I clothed myself up very well here and when I left he owed me seven dollars which he was to pay in a short time. There was a camp meeting in Dillen's Settlement while I was at work here to which Mr. Morris & wife & myself went. It was at the same place where I joined the Methodist last year. We had a good time here again for which I was hectored severely by Phelps & some others afterwards who did not believe in the Doctrine.

While Here I first became acquainted with Charles C. Rich[72] & his fathers family about whom we will speak more by & by. Charles was then an uncommon civil steady, honest young man but made no pretentions to religion & I soon had a great regard and attachment for him.

While at Mr. Morris Phelps I attended a meeting in Pleasant Grove for the purpose of forming a Temperance Society got up by Neil Johnson, a brother to Archabald, my teacher.[73] He was the most eloquent preacher in all the country and now spoke loud and long against the practice of drinking ardent spirits and I was quite overcome by his arguments and altogether converted & after meeting he called for volunteers to join the Temperance cause & I and 14 others came forward and gave our name as members. Drinking to excess was a thing which I never had even any temptation for and although I love a dram sometimes yet seldom ever drink when I have it by me Notwithstanding all that, [I am] constitutionally temperate. Yet I here joined the Temperance Society to be reformed from drinking and at the time did not ever expect to taste another drop of ardent spirits again in my life what an absurdity after all was over I pondered deeply on the subject and continually felt like I wanted a dram yet firm in my resolution not to drink again. That night I dreamed a man handed me a bottle of whiskey & I drank deep. In the morning I still wanted some & did for days during which time I had the offer but refused It was a mystery to me why I so wanted it now for the first time in all my life and that after I had set out not to drink any more, but "when the law came sin revived" I suppose.

Mr. Morris Phelps and all his neighbours thought very little of all this and came very near making me sick of my bargain for it did look foolish to me to quit that which I never did.

While here [Willow Springs] I went over to Peoria, then called Fort Clark.[74] It was a beautiful town site with only one or two log houses on it but did not look anything like a town. The remains of an old fort was still there. Lake Peoria lay on the East of the site and is a most beautiful sheet of water formed by a sudden expansion of the Illinois river. It terminates at the lower part of the town site where there was a ferry. The river here is verry narrow.

When I was done work for Mr. Morris Phelps I went to see Anna and from thence returned to Stout's Grove again well clothed except shoes. I staid here some time and then set in with Mr. Jonas Hittle of Mackinaw town to work at a mill which he was now building on the Mackinaw just above town He had a number of hands at work we had a jolly time all worked well He was a fine man to work for done well by his hands & gave them plenty to eat and was liberal He [Jonas Hittle] furnished whiskey for his men every morning it being necessary for we had to work in the water sometimes. At first I was too conscientious to drink for which I was dully rallied by the rest who considered it worse than folly & nonsense for a sober temperate man to be under any obligations not to drink when it was for his health, & I thought so too. The temperance regulations allowed a man to use ardent spirits as medicine & recollecting this one morning I took the jug and called the attention of the company who had assembled for the purpose of taking their morning dram, to witness that I took it as medicine at which all shouted applause & after this I always used it as I thought proper & have never since been priest bound on that subject nor done any harm in drinking on my own descretion This closes the history of my temperance society career for I never troubled myself any more about the Temperance cause.

I worked some more than a month at Mr. Hittles & then went to Stouts Grove and set in with Mr. Watson to mow his hay While grinding the sythe I was taken with a severe attack of the fever which was followed by a hard spell of sickness. Mr. Watson becoming alarmed about me, sent to Hodson's after Anna who came and attended on me faithfully. I was sick some time with a fever untill I was very much reduced & weak and feeble The fever was succeeded by the chill fever[75] & this continued to reduce me for a long time during which time I went to Mr. Mathew Robb's to stay, Anna still with me.[76]

While at Mr Watson's, there was a weding to come off at Mr Jonathan Hodges, whose daughter Sarah was to be married to John Ament. Sarah was one of my school mates last summer & we had now become very intimate & she had long since told me all her expectations about marrying and in fact she was a girl of the very first quality. I & Anna attended the weding While there I had a chill & was very sick with a high fever & was out of my senses most of the night. All else went off joyful & gay and all seemed to enjoy themselves except Ebenezer Mitchel another school mate who had always untill a few days since expected to get this fair damsel himself. He was here & look bad enough while she was on the floor as all remarked. He was a dull stupid unsuspecting fellow and had been fairly duped by her.

I had some hopes of soon being well while at Mr Robbs but was taken with a relapse, which was worse than the first spell. This came near using me up for I was now unable to walk around.

Anna took a notion that if I could get to Dillen's Settlement that I would soon get well & so Mr Robb took us there where I staid all winter [1830] having a chill & fever every day I became so stupid that I would not move from the fire when my clothes would scorch till they would smoke. It is incredible what a stupifying effect that fell disease will have on anyone. I was at several different places while here this winter & experienced & tasted the very dregs of adversity for some places I was not welcome & I knew it & could not get away & who knows the disagreeable feeling to be in such a condition but those who have experienced it.

Some time this winter Anna went to see Mr. Phelps to collect the amout coming to me which he promised to pay to her on a certain day in Pekin, and she went to get it and he did not come & we learned afterwards that he disappointed her purposly for he expected to move away shortly and cheat me out of it which thing a Mr. Sanford Porter[77] a neighbour of his knowing the circumstances took up for me and made him pay him and he afterwards paid it to Anna.

I will mention one man who seemed to express the warmest friendship and hospitality towards me while there sick and that was Mr William Eads.[78] I started out to return to Stouts Grove on foot in the spring and came to his house and he objected to my going because he said I was not able & seemed such a warm friend & so willing [for me] to stay that I tarried longer I had been at his house in the winter and staid some week & was treated well. I never could forget his goodness to me in this one of the times of my greatest afflictions & deepest distress when a friend is so much needed and such a warm friend, in the midst of calamity, when all the world is cold and regardless to your wants how good and consoling it is.

I went from Mr. Eads' and traveled on foot towards Little mackinaw to Stouts Grove. When I left Mr. Eads' I had not had the chills for some time & thought I could walk to Stouts Grove by taking this rout for I could stop occasionally.

I went about 12 miles the first day it being very warm and pleasant but at night I had a light chill again. The next morning I felt very bad & hardly able to walk but I went on to my Uncle Samuels' about four miles [at Little Mackinaw], where I found them all well & glad to see me. Tonight I had the chill again which increased now and began to bring me down. I staid here a day or two, while here I went to see my father & Allen, Sally [Sarah] & Lydia who lived nearby and found them all well.

I got an opportunity of going to Stouts Grove on horseback, with Saml. Stout jr. who was going there so I ventured & we set out and was overtaken by a rain storm & had to ride hard to get in without a wetting. We put up at Uncle Davids who lived in this grove now and that night I had a sever[e] turn of chill & fever & was out of my se[n]ses but they were very kind to me & done for me all they could.

I had now arrived to the place whence I started and felt myself at home. I went around as I was able to visit my old neighbors & friends all who seemed glad to see me & treated me well but still I was troubled with lingering chills & fevers for a long time.

◆ 1831 ◆

The last winter was the hardest winter known in Illinois.[79] The corn crops were not geathered The snow was uncommonly deep & people suffered extremely. Hardly able to geather corn to, feed their stock & get their wood. For me I had the chill fever all winter which gave me the full enjoyment of its cooling effects. It is to this day well known by the name of the "cold winter"

This summer was likewise very cold and crops yielded uncommonly poor. Such as was never known in this country.

After I had made my visits to my friends not being able to do any work I commenced going to school to Mr. Porter[80] who was teaching here & boarded at Mr. Jonathan Hodges where I staid all summer. Here I finished my education which only consisted in a knowledge of Reading, Writing, Arithmetic, English Grammar, Geography and a tolerable insite of Logic. All excep the last I had a good knowledge and for these times was a good education.

Towards the latter part of the season I began to feel like I could labor again and accordingly set in to do work for Mr. Watson Mowing. I worked untill noon the first day and came in with another chill & was again laid low with the chill fever. I was now entirely disheartened and almost dispaired ever again being able to support myself During this Spell of Sickness I was but an expense again on my friends who however took good care of me, and rendered my situation as comfortable as possible.

Sometime this summer my father took Allen and went down the Illinois [River] to parts unknown to any of the rest of us which was the last I heard of them for years.[81]

Stout's Grove, which had been famous for religion was now filled with jars and contentions about the "Non-essentials" as they termed some of the different tenats but sufficiently essential to keep them in a perpetual quarrel which nearly extinguished my religious fire no[t] believing that any good was in such spirits as they manifested.

There was annother Camp meeting this fall here at which many very able preachers attended and made an uncommon effort to convert sinners to no effect The fact was their internal broils had resulted in a perfect want of confidence in each other and all these things were well known to the sinners who did not believe in them.

This fall I recovered from my sickness again so that I commenced work and had tolerable success for awhile and again bright hopes arose & I began to form schemes to acquire property and make a respectable living.

◆ 1832 ◆

I lived with Col. Robert McClure[82] this winter He was a kind and obliging man My prospects were now very good and I felt cheerful and happy But my joy was again to be turned in to sorrow and dispair for toward the latter part of the winter I was again taken down with a chill and was for three days perfectly delerious and by all the neighbors given up to die.

After I had recovered my senses I was so much reduced that I could not sit up. This was the severest spell of sickness I had ever had but did not last long for I soon recovered so as to go around & in a short time felt quite well but without the hopes of ever being able to labor for a living.

My friends now advised me to take up a school as they said I could do better at that business which would spare my health. This I concluded to do as a last and forlorn hope to a respectable living [for] which a natural backwardness almost disqualified me. Moreover I was now very destitute of clothing and in fact could not make a respectable appearance among strangers. However by turning the avails of a colt which I had sold to Mr. Watson I made out to fix myself for the intended "Voyage" and earley in spring I set out accompanied by Benjamin Conger[83] who was going along for the purpose of going to school to me. I was now fairly well launched out into the world having about 14 dollars in cash & but a poor outfit in clothing.

We travelled north to the Walnut Grove[84] about 12 miles and staid all night at Hon. James Bird's with whom we were well acquainted. Here we had faint hopes of raising a school but found no chance for every one was busily engaged in putting in their crops and at the best cared but too little about educating their children We went on the next day wending our way North but did not go far before Conger proposed going West down the Illinois river arguing that the best prospects were in that direction, to which I consented & travelled till noon took dinner & he was now quite home sick & dispaired of us ever doing any thing and so he turned in towards Mackinaw town & I journeyed to Dillon's Settlement to see my two sisters Anna & Lydia Here I tried for a school as some were desirious to have one while others did not. After several days of suspense I failed.

I now began to think that I could not raise a school at this season of the year and upon the failure of this school I was left entirely discouraged and knew not what to do. I felt like I was totally abandoned to eternal disappointment, poverty and disgrace. Nothing but dark forebodings in view I retired to the broad prairie and sat down & wept bitterly and there alone & aloud mourned my hard fortune for a long time I felt that my life was only the sport of misfortune and sorrow After giving vent to my feelings I determined to leave entirely the land of my acquaintance & bad misfortunes & throw myself in the midst of strangers & see if a change of fortune would follow Knowing it could not well be worse. But where to go I knew not.

While there I wrote the following letter to my sister Anna & left it with my little sister Lydia giving her instructions to give it to Anna herself & not to let anyone see it as I felt that my situation was perfectly disgraceful & was not willing for it to be known.

Tazwell County
Dillon's Settlement
April 5th, 1832.

Dear Sister,

This is to let you know the situation I am in at present.

I have tried to get a school in this settlement, but failed.

What I shall do next I know not. It seems that misfortune comes upon me at every attempt to make an honest & respectable living. And if I can not make an honest living I am resolved not to live at all.

I hope that Heaven may direct me in the way I should go.

I am resolved to live respectable if I do live

I am now in the prairie not knowing where to go

I hope you will not be disheartened if I leave the country.

If I stay here I can make nothing.

I will go wherever I think I can do the best and write you when I stop.

If I stay here I am compassed with sickness and poverty & I do not see how much worse I can be off anywhere else.

If I labor, sickness is sure to follow If I try any other way to make a livelihood I am attended with disappointment which is worse than sickness. What shall I do? I feel like a poor out cast without a friend to council or assist me or even to communicate my troubles to.

May the Lord guide my steps in the right way and dispose of me as he sees best.

If I knew what to do gladly would I drop my pen & do it quickly.

When I shall see you I know not, but do the best you can till then.

The day may come when prosperity may be in my favor & I enjoy life & peace better than I do now.


No more. Your affectionate brother.

Hosea Stout.

After committing the above to my little sister I then went to Pekin, a town on the Illinois river & now the County seat of Tazwell County, with an intention of going with Col. R. McClure, who was going down the river to purchase a lot of seed corn. The corn last year being not ripe the whole country had to go south for seed corn, this spring. When I arrived at Pekin I found that McClure had just left, so that I was again disappointed. My intention in going with him was that if I met with no opportunity of getting into business I might at least learn something about the ways of the world [of] which I knew myself to be grossly ignorant & at the same time I knew that McClure would do anything he could to advance my interest. I found my calculations again futile.

I was now very unwell & hardly able to go about notwithstanding I went on travelling up the river & by falling in with Mr. Holland who had a waggon I rode home with him some 15 miles that night at Holland's Grove again intending to try my fortune to the North.

Mr. Holland tryed to disuade me from going North not believing I could get a school & I had not much hopes myself But being unable to labor I went on the next day to one of my old acquaintance's William Burt on Crow Creek where I staid all night [Here I] was well treated and encouraged in my undertaking. He [William Burt] lived in Stouts grove during my last sickness this spring & from whom I had recieved kind attention.

The next day I went on to the Ox-Bow Prairie where I made my intentions and business known to two men who gave me encouragements of raising a school and refered me to Mr Asahel Hannum who they said could decide the case for me.[85] This was on Sabbath. I went to see Mr. Hannum & made known my business, who was in favor of a school after very closely criticizing me as to my ability which I believe was to his satisfaction.

He was a very stern man & yet kind & hospitable to me. I staid all night with him & in the morning drew up my article and went around the settlement to procure subscribers.

Suffice it to say that I succeeded in making up a small school here, which was to commence the next Monday. I boarded at Mr. Hannum's untill then and was well treated by him

During this week I became acquainted with nearly all the men in this place by going to a rail making frolic at Mr. Harts, & was well pleased with them as a general thing

My school commenced and I done well for a short time & I believe to the satisfaction of all.

It is well known by all that the Black Hawk War broke out this spring [1832] which after the exaggerated reports of Maj. Stillmans defeat raised such an excitement through this section of country that nearley all business was suspended.[86] We were called upon to defend ourselves being the frontier county (Putnam) and one company raised to rainge and patrol the country, which for a short time left us in the enjoyment of peace.

I was never untill now brought sufficiently near the scenes of war to know what effect it would have on me. I had often heard its horrors portrayed. Often had I heard the demorilizing effect a soldiers life had upon people, all of which I desired to escape. I had yet great religious concern of mind & desired exceedingly to know how to make my calling & election sure & well knowing my own weakness in resisting evil I feared this demorilizing effect of a campaign even if I should escape the scalping knife now so much spoken of together with the horid accounts of Still-mans defeat.

These things caused me deep trouble which however I kept consealed from others.

On the contrary I deeply felt the necessity of rallying to the aid of my country & running my chance with the rest. I was certainly as pure and devoted a patriot as ever was.

I felt that the interest of my country was above every thing else & I must defend it at the risk of my life & supposed that every one felt the same I did not even suspect that our rulers were full of the political intrigues which I afterwards learned

So upon the whole I was now perfectly uncontaminated.

With all these inocent feelings I attended a second call for more rain-gers at which the whole entire Regiment turned out & I with the rest not however without undergoing a considerable change of heart for the evil effects of a campaign & the scalping knife had both lost its terror to me & I only desired to march to meet the enemy such is the effect of martial music & warlike speech on the mind of man.

My school was suspended & I engaged with the rest in our rainging excursions from Hennepin the County seat down the river some twenty miles.

This was the line to be guarded All to the West of the river at this point was evacuated by the whites

This new life suited me well for my health had now been on the gain & I was well able to do all the duties of a soldier.

Some time passed thus in the mean time we built a fort in the Ox Bow prairie where all the inhabitants fled for safety

Some men were often so terrified that they could not be got to stand guard. False alarms were frequent & I often saw people ready to abandon the fort to the Indians for their own safety.

I found that people were not so purely patriotic as I expected

During the time of my service the Indians made a decent on some men who had gone to look to their farms about 15 miles from Hennepin and killed a man named Phillips & at another they killed some 15 persons [named] Halls & Pedigrews & carried two young Miss Halls captive.[87]

These things created a great excitement. The people in Pekin even forti-fied themselves.

It is not needful for me to go into detail on this subject.

Once during the war I made a visit to Stouts grove and back again

This war was ended after the battle of Bad-ax & I returned to Stouts grove and tarried awhile & again in the fall returned to the Ox-Bow & took up another school for the term of three months, without any thing of particular importance transpiring except some three or four weddings & the two Miss Halls who had been taken captive by the Indians had now returned & were in this settlement. They were afterwards married to two brothers named Munson.[88]

After my school was out I returned to Stouts Grove again & now in good circumstances & tolerable plenty of money & uncommon good health.

From here I set out for Dillon's Settlement to see Anna & Lydia as I had not hard anything particular about them since I left in the Spring.

Upon arriving there I heard that she [Anna] was married & upon arriving at the place where Lydia was I heard that she [Anna] was married to a mormon widower who had five children.[89]

This perfectly astonished me & I at first felt like simply going to see her for the purpose of telling my mind and then leaving her forever for I considered it a disgrace beyond endurance to be any way connected with the mormons & a widower too was too bad.

I had only heard the gold Bible stories & the fortifying [of] Jackson county Mo[90] & in short the common and universal slang then going about them & did not even once think but it was true.

I thought deep all that night intending to morrow to see her for the last time. My agitation of mind was intense but on my way the next day I came to the more sober conclusion not to unbosom my feeling for as she was now fairly into a scrape not to irritate her feelings but let her enjoy herself if she could so I now hastened on with this view.

When I arrived there I was met by her & introduced to Mr Jones who seemed glad to see me & in fact was a very clever & pleasant man against whom I could find no fault and had he not been a Mormon [I] should have been well enough pleased with [him]. But O! the stigma & disgrace inevitable to that name [Mormon]. This bore on my mind & weighed down my feelings while I endeavored to put on a cheerful & happy countenance. The subject of religion was not mentioned to me while I at the same time was anxious to go into an investigation of it.

I found them living on Farm Creek. He [Benjamin Jones] was engaged at a saw mill with N. Wixom.[91] This mill I assisted to build while I worked for Morris Phelps two years ago.

I staid here several days, during which time I saw C. C. Rich who was now a Mormon Elder. We spent several days together all of which time was spent investigating our religious tenats.

Suffice it to say that we passed over the grounds of our different belief, refering our opinions wherever we differed to the Bible.

It is not necessary to mention our investigation which resulted in all cases in the loss of my position while he always sustained his on the fairest possible terms.

The perplexity which this threw me into can only be realized by those who has been through the same thing with the same anticipations before them that I had. I saw plainly that my positions were wrong & did also verily believe Mormonism to be correct.

All my plans & calculations both spiritually and temporally were now futile. The agitation of my mind was intense & I did not know what to do.

I could not forego the idea of joining the church for aside from the disgrace which would follow I was fearful least I should not live up to its precepts as I did with the methodists. I wanted confidence in myself

After remaining here [Farm Creek] untill I had fairly investigated Mormonism & also [I] became acquainted with a number of Mormons whose society I was very fond but did not express it I returned to Stouts Grove where I commenced preaching the doctrine to the astonishment of all who knew me, yet at the same time [I] did not profess to believe it.

I was astonished at myself when I saw with what ease & fluency I could confute any one who would oppose me.

This raised a considerable excitement in the grove.

Emboldened by my success I soon made it in my way to attack even the ministers who I believed did not understand the Scriptures & I also thought I had always the best of their arguments.

Matters rested in this way while I made several visits back and forth to Jones always with one or two new mormon ideas to argue on my return to the grove.

This winter I took up a school in the [Stout's] grove at which I done a very good business.[92]

◆ 1833 ◆

After my school was out I went up North near crow creek to Mr. Joseph Phillips and set in with him to raise a crop with him where I spent the summer without any thing of importance transpiring more than my studdying the principals of mormonism as I had opportunity from some mormons near the mouth of Crow Creek.[93] I raised here a good crop of corn.

I made several visits to the [Stout's] grove in the summer & after my crop was laid by I returned to Farm Creek to Benjamin Jones my brother-in-law.

About this time Mr. Nathan Wixom the owner of the Farm Creek saw mill wishing to move North to a more new Country proposed to sell out his mill & improvements to Jones & myself.

We accordingly b[o]ught him out for six hundred dollars. Sep 2nd[94]

We were to pay one third of the lumber we sawed untill the mill was paid for. This was a very fair opportunity for us for the rent of a saw mill in those days was one third while we could apply it on the payment

I now had a permanent home living with my brother-in law

Shortly after I came here to live I had a severe attack of chill fever & was sick several weeks.

After recovering I returned to Mr. Phillips & geathered my corn & sold it to Wixom in part payment for the mill

During the time I was here Mr. Phillips died. He had been failing all summer.

It was while I was here on the night of the 13th of Nov. that the notable Meteoric shower took place about which so much has been said which happened while the mormons were driven out of Jackson County Missouri and now in the open fields. They hailed this as one of the signs of the Last days.

I confess I did not know what to think of it. The sight was magnificent & grand.[95]

After I returned home from Mr. Phillip's I was busily engaged with Jones in the affairs of the sawmill in procuring logs &c in time for business in the spring.

Here I was well suited with the society I was in. There was mormon meetings once a week to which I attended and became intimate with the doctrines they professed & did most devoutly believe it. but I must confess that I was afraid to join them least I should not hold out faithful & thus make my situation worse.

There was also good society here [Farm Creek] who were not mormons with all I became acquainted & in short was well suited with the people who resided here.

It is hardly necessary for me to record the fluctuating feelings which I necessarily had to encounter between mormonism & the popular sects of the day for every one who had embraced mormonism has, I suppose experienced the same thing.

I now assumed a more business-like life and soon became well known in the country around here which ends this year.

### ✦ 1834 ✦

We done good business this season with the mill & in the fall I found my-self in comfortable circumstances.

This summer the Zion Camp marched up to Missouri to retake Jackson County under Joseph Smith jr. the Prophet.[96]

Hyrum Smith[97] Lyman Wight[98] & others passed by here on their way up to Jackson County & staid several days during which time they preached several times here.

The effect of their preaching was powerful on me & when I considered that they were going up to Zion to fight for their lost inheritances under the special directions of God it was all that I could do to refrain from going. Jones and I let them have one yoke of oxen.

Elder Charles C. Rich went with them.

The events of this expedition is so well known that I need say nothing about it.

Several were added to the mormon Church here this summer.

So ends this year.

### ✦ 1835 ✦

We spent the past winter in cutting & drawing a large number of saw logs to the mill preparitory for the spring and also in getting out and selling a large quantity of hewed timber for the Peoria market at which we done a good & profitable business. We kept some six or eight hands hired at this time.

Early in the spring we purchased an interest in a mill then building on Crow Creek in Putnam County for one hundred & fifty dollars

There was two mill seats on this stream one owned by Jos. Martin & the other by Hadlock & Hunter. We bought out Hunter's share which was one half.

This was about one quarter of a mile below Martin's mill & in order to raise water [we] had to back water on him while he was trying to bluff us & thus obtain his mill seat.

In this case we bought with our mill seat also a law-suit[99] as will be hereafter seen. We also sold our Farm Creek mill to Jacob Hepperley.[100]

# Autobiography of Hosea Stout

## 1810 TO 1844[101]

Hosea Stout son of Joseph and Anna Stout, who [Joseph] was the son of Samuel Stout, who was the son of Peter Stout, was born in the County of Mercer and State of Kentucky, near a small Shaker village called Pleasant Hill, on the 18th day of September 1810 and in the spring of the year 1819, removed with his parents to Clinton County Ohio and there on the 28th day of July 1824 his mother died and the following fall he went to Wilmington the County seat of Clinton and lived with Isiah Morris, and his father removed with his family to Cincinnati Ohio from thence to Louisville Kentucky, from thence to Missouri from thence to Illinois, leaving him [Hosea] with Mr. Morris, where he stayed untill the spring of 1826 when he left Mr. Morris and went and lived with Eli Harvey, who was a member of the Society of Quakers. he made his home there untill the summer of 1828 when he removed to with Stephen Stout his cousin, to Tazewell County Illinois, and remained in that vicinity untill the spring of the year April 5th 1832 when he went to Putnam County [Illinois] and there took up a school in what is called the Ox Bow prairie and after he had continued his school about one month there came orders from Govornor John Reynolds for a company of volunteers to be raised to guard the frontiers of Putnam County against the invasions of the Sac & Fox Indians then at war with the whites on the North East parts of Illinois, and he dismissed his school and volunteered in what was termed the "Putnam County volunteers" where he continued as a Ranger untill near the close of the war when he returned back to Tazewell County and in the fall went back to Putnam County and again took up a school for a term of three months, after which he returned back to Tazewell and there took up another school for three months and in the Spring went to Putnam County and raised a crop with a Mr. Joseph Phillips, and in the fall which was in the year 1833 he went to the west part of Tazewell County, about 3 miles East of Peoria on Farm Creek and there, in Company with Benjamin Jone, who had marrid his sister Anna, purchased a saw mill where he continued untill the Spring of 1835 when they sold their mill and they in Company with Samuel Hadlock built another saw mill in the south of Putnam County near the mouth of and on Crow Creek. While he resided on Farm Creek he became acquainted with the Latter Day Saints whose doctrine he believed the first time he ever heard it advanced. They remained in company [Hosea, Benjamin Jones, and Samuel Hadlock] untill in the fall of 1836. He then went to Tazewell County about 3 miles below their old saw mill to a Town on the Bank of the Illinois river Called Wesley City, where he went at the carpenters business in company with Benjm Jones untill in August 1837 when he and Mr Jones and several more families, who had also sold out for the same purpose, went to Caldwell County Missouri, for the purpose of being geathered with and associating with the Latter Day saints, where he purchased 200 acres of good tilable land and built him a house, and commenced opening a farm,[102] He there became acquainted with and married Surmantha Peck, the daughter of Benjamin and Phebe Peck, on the 7th day of January 1838 on the 26th day of August following he was baptized into the Church of Jesus Christ of Latter Day Saints by Elder Charles C. Rich, this was in the time that the mob was harrasing the church and the brethren were then under arms to defend themselves against the voilence of the mob. He entered the war with the rest of his brethren and was in all the difficulties, which they passed through in Caldwell & Davisse Counties, with the mob.[103] On the morning of 26 day of October he was called upon while at home by one of the brethren, to go with a company, under the command of David W. Patten[104] to rescue some of our brethren who had been taken prisoner by a company of the mob under Capt Samuel Bogard [Bogart] then stationed on Crooked river about 4 miles west from his house, who they intended to put to death unless they should deny the doctrine of the Latter Day Saints.[105] When they had come near the place where it was supposed the mob were encamped the company dismounted and fastened their horses to a fence and divided their compay into two parties one under David W. Patten and the other under Charles C. Rich, and proceeded to the place where it was thought they were, Captain Rich taking a cirtuous rout came in the rear that they might be surrounded before they were aware of their approach. They pursued their course to the place previously designated and there met but the mob not being there, they left a few men to guard the place where they had met and the Company marched on the road towards Crooked river which was near by in search of Bogards Company. They did not proceed far in that direction before they were hailed by somebody from behind a tree a few words passed and the man who was behind the tree fired and brought one of Pattens men to the ground, whose name was Obanion [Patrick O'Banion], who died that day. They then found that they were in the borders of Bogards Camp, the brethren pushed forward, being incenced at the treatment which they had received, and in a few moments were fired upon by Bogards whole company who were at this time within a few yards of D. W. Patten's Company. Patten ordered a charge which was made instantly and a severe and bloody conflict ensued which did not however last but a few moments, for Bogard, and the greatest part of his men, fled on the approch of the brethren. They were situated behind the bank of the river and had a fair view of the brethren, who were approaching from the East, and it being at the dawn of day [Bogart's company] could distinctly see them whereas they [Bogart's company] were almost entirely out of sight. The brethren rushed into their midst and sword in hand put to death every one who came in their way, all of Bogards company who did not run away with him were killed in a few moments. The mob had to make their retreat by running through croocked river at a place where the water was waist deep and before they could get across the brethren were on the bank, and many a mobber was there baptised without faith or repentance under the messingers of lead sent by the brethren and summoned to appear and give an account of his sewardship which was terminated in an attempt to murder those who will Judge them at the Great day.[106] Some as they were crossing the river would exclaim "we are brethren," to stay the brethren untill they could escape. In the first onset D. W. Patten was mortally wounded, and the command fell on Captain Rich The brethren had three killed and six wounded, the names of those who were killed were David W. Patten Patterson Obanion and Gideon Carter. The names of those who were wounded were Eli Chase, Norman Shearer, Curtis Hodges sr Arthur Millikin, Jos Holbrook and James Hendrix who had the cords of his neck cut with a ball which deprived him of the use of his limbs and he was found lying with his head down hill unable to help himself or even move hand or foot but could speak as well as ever, William Seeley one of the prisoners whom the mob had taken was Shot through the breast by them on the first approach of the brethren and was found with the blood running out of his mouth.[107] David W. Patten lived to be taken about 6 miles from the field of battle and died, at Br. Stephen Winchester's[108] The mob lost according to the best calculation which could be made by the brethren about 30, or forty men,[109] the rest fled in every direction through Clay and Ray Counties reporting as they went that they had been attacted by the mormons and the whole of their Company killed and they alone was left to tell the tale. This created a great excitement throughout those counties and Govornor Boggs issued his order to exterminate the mormons or drive them from the State and made a demand for all those who had been in the Battle of Croocked river who were to be tried for murder. There was ten thousand men raised by order of the Govornor to put his exterminating order into execution and arrest those who had been in the battle[110] and on the 28th day of Oct General Lucas with about three thousand men encamped near Far-West and demanded the leaders of the Church and also the brethren aforesaid upon the refusal of which he would sack and pillage the City. After several communications had passed between the parties, Presidents Joseph Smith jr Hyrum Smith, Sidney Rigdon, Parley P. Pratt, Lyman Wight, and George W. Robinson were delivered into the hands of the mob through the treacherous influence of G. M. Hinkle John Corrill, Reed Peck & some other false brethren.[111] Resistance was now too late and all who had been in the Battle of Crooked river plainly saw what they had to expect. There was no alternative for them but to escape or fall into the hands of their enemies who had sworn their destruction consequently on the night of which the above named brethren was given into the hands of the mob, which was the 31st day of October, twenty seven of them made their escape about mid-night and proceeded north and at the dawn of day were crossing Grand river about one mile above Adam ondi Ahman, among which number was the subject of this narrative.[112] The account of the troubles of the brethren are not connected with his history and therefore will not be proper in this place. They continued their course North throug a howling wilderness, for eleven days when they arived at the settlements of the whites near the rapids of the Des Moines river in the Teritory of Iowa. The company however divided before they came to the settlement in order to avoid any excitement which might be created by so many men being together.

When they left Far West and for two days after the wether was very warm and pleasant on the third day after they left a deep snow fell and the weather turned exceedingly cold and many of them being thinly clad suffered beyond description, from having to face the Northern winds.

Their provisions likewise soon gave out and it was very seldom that they could procure any wild game, and they were near upon perishing of cold and hunger. The company which he was in came to the Mississippi river the next day after the other had crossed and from the increace of the running ice could not cross, and leaving one of their number Br R. [Robert] B. Thompson with some [one with] whom he was acquainted went to the Quincy ferry which took them two days, and not being able to cross went back into the country and worked for their board two days after however sending Charles C. Rich over the river in a canoe.

When they arrived at the Quincy ferry they met some of their brethren from Caldwell County and learned the fate of the church[113] but got no satisfactory accounts from their families They crossed the river and found some brethren who treated them kindly, where also some of their company came soon after, and they had the satisfaction of meeting each other once more when they were not exposed to mob violence. Several of the brethren then took a job of cutting cord wood on the islands just above Quincy where they had the pleasure of each other's society [un]interupted and could receive the news from Far West as the brethren emegrated to Illinois; He there remained untill his wife came from Missouri, whe[re] they met each other in good health and spirits.[114] They then moved about four miles East from Quincy to the Missionary Institute and remained there untill in April, then moved to Payson about 14 miles South East from Quincy and worked at the carpenters trade for a support during which time his wife was mostly confined to her bed in consequence of the exposures she had endured from the troubles in Missour and in removing to Illinois in the month of February. He remained there untill the 5th day of August following and then removed to Lee County Iowa, stopping about one week in Quincy. His wife was still very feeble and on the 29th day of November 1839 she died [in Lee County, Iowa]. In the month of March 1840 [he] removed to Nauvoo, Illinois[115] He was ordained an elder[116] in the Church of Christ at the General Conference[117] of said Church held at Nauvoo October the 5th 1839 under the hands of Elder Seymoure Brunson.[118]

On the 8th of March 1840 he was appointed Clerk for the High Council[119] of the Church of Jesus Christ of Latter Day Saints, at Nauvoo

On the 16th day of May 1840 he was elected to the office of Second Lieutenant in the company of Light Infantry of volunteers in the second Batalion of the fifty ninth Regiment of Illinois militia at the organization of the said Company in Nauvoo.

On the 29th day of November following he was married to Louisa Taylor daughter of William and Elizabeth Taylor.

On Thursday the 4th day of February 1841 the Nauvoo Legion[120] was organized by electing the general officers of the same as follows Joseph Smith Lieutenant General John C. Bennett[121] Major General, Wilson Law[122] Brigadier General first Cohort, & D. C. Smith[123] Brigadier General Second Cohort the company aforesaid [the company of Light Infantry of volunteers in the Second Battalion of the Fifty-Ninth Regiment of Illinois Militia] was then and there placed [as] the Second Company first Batalion first Regiment Second Cohort Nauvoo Legion and the captain A. P. Rockwood[124] appointed Drill officer of the Legion with the rank of Colonel, and on the Saturday following he [Hosea] was elected Captain of said company to fill the vacancy of A. P. Rockwood

On the fourth day of September following he [Hosea] was elected Major of the Second Batalion first Regiment as aforesaid.

On the 20th of May 1843, the Court Martial of the Nauvoo Legion[125] passed a Resolution that the second Batallion as aforesaid should be organized into a Regiment of Light Infantry, which was numbered the fifth Regiment Second Cohort Nauvoo Legion which was organized on the 23rd day of June following and he was then elected Colonel of the same which he commanded as such during the war which was waged against the saints in June 1844 in which our beloved Prophet & seer Joseph Smith and Patriarch Hyrum Smith fell martyrs to the cause of God while the honor of the Governor and faith of the State [Illinois] was pledged for their safety.[126]

On the fourth day of October 1844 he was ordained an Elder in the Quorums of Seventies[127] under the hands of Henry Jacobs, Benjm L. Clapp[128] and Samuel Brown[129] Presidents in said Quorums, and at the General Conference on the 8th day of said month he was ordained one of the Presidents & Clerk of the Eleventh Quorum of the Seventies upon nomination of President Brigham Young under the hands of Presidents Brigham Young and Amasa Lyman[130] at the organization of said Quorum.

# Notes

## INTRODUCTION TO THE 1962 EDITION BY REED STOUT

1.  Joseph Smith, *History of the Church of Jesus Christ of Latter-day Saints* (Salt Lake City, 1902), I, 166.

2.  The Doctrine and Covenants of the Church of Jesus Christ of Latter-Day Saints (Salt Lake City, 1954), Sec. 47.

3.  "General Epistle from the Council of the Twelve Apostles to the Church of Jesus Christ of Latter-day Saints, abroad, dispersed throughout the Earth,..." written at Winter Quarters and signed by Brigham Young, December 23, 1847, in behalf of the Quorum of the Twelve Apostles. *The Latter-day Saints Millennial Star,* X (Liverpool, England, 1848), 85.

4.  The Hosea Stout journals and autobiographies have been the basis for a biography written by Wayne Stout, *Hosea Stout, Utah's Pioneer Statesman* (Salt Lake City, 1953) and have supplied material for a family history by the same author entitled *Our Pioneer Ancestors, Genealogical and Biographical Histories of the Cox-Stout Families* (Salt Lake City, 1944). The Hosea Stout journals have also been referred to and quoted in numerous articles appearing in periodicals and various books concerned with western and Mormon history. Among such books may be mentioned Bernard DeVoto, *The Year of Decision: 1846* (Boston, 1943); Preston Nibley, *Exodus to Greatness* (Salt Lake City, 1947); Juanita Brooks, *The Mountain Meadows Massacre* (Stanford, 1950); Dale L. Morgan, ed., *The Overland Diary of James A. Pritchard from Kentucky to California in 1849* (San Francisco, 1959); LeRoy Hafen and Ann W. Hafen, *Handcarts to Zion* (Glendale, 1960).

5.  Juanita Brooks has written numerous articles on the subject of Utah and the West appearing in the *Utah Historical Quarterly, Western Humanities Review,* and other periodicals. She is the author of *The Mountain Meadows Massacre* (Stanford, 1950) and *John Doyle Lee, Zealot—Pioneer Builder—Scapegoat* (Glendale, 1961), and

co-editor of *A Mormon Chronicle: The Diaries of John D. Lee, 1846–1876* (San Marino, 1955).

6.  Concerning Hosea Stout and the autobiography, John Henry Evans wrote in *Charles Coulson Rich, Pioneer Builder of the West* (New York, 1936), 21, "His narrative…of his life, which has never been published, is strangely fascinating, and reads like an impossible tale. And it is beautifully told, with great simplicity.…

    "Stout had some rare gifts. A student by nature, he observed men and events with curious scrutiny. His mind was keen and penetrating. He was particularly concerned with mathematics. Always industrious as well as ambitious, he had gone to school more than most Westerners of the period."

# THE AUTOBIOGRAPHY OF HOSEA STOUT, 1810 TO 1835

1.  Hosea Stout's paternal grandfather was Samuel Stout, born April 10, 1740, in Lancaster, Pennsylvania, a son of Peter Stout, a Quaker who moved with his family in 1762 to a Quaker settlement on Cane Creek in Orange County, North Carolina. On October 10, 1762, Samuel Stout married Rachel Chancy (or Chauncey), and about 1786 moved to Tennessee, but returned to North Carolina in 1792. Samuel Stout's son Joseph, was father of Hosea.

2.  The years in which events occurred in the lives of members of Hosea Stout's family are inserted by interlineations in the autobiography, but they do not appear to be in his handwriting. Moreover, the years as inserted are not always correct. Since these do not appear to have been supplied by Hosea Stout, the years here shown in brackets have been corrected where incorrect, and the full dates, where known, have been added.

3.  Pleasant Smith was Hosea's maternal grandmother. She was a sister of Rachel Chancy, Hosea Stout's paternal grandmother (the wife of Samuel Stout). She married Daniel Smith, who died in 1791.

4.  It is highly likely that the "army" in which Joseph Stout enlisted was the Tennessee militia. Frustrated by the unwillingness or inability of the federal government to protect them from Indian attacks in the mid-1790s, residents of the Southwest Territory, which included East Tennessee, formed militias to repel the attacks.

5.  Mercer County, formed in 1786, is in the bluegrass region of Kentucky. The county seat, Harrodsburg, founded in 1774, was the first permanent English settlement west of the Allegheny Mountains.

6.  Shaker is the name commonly given to members of the religious sect properly named "The United Society of Believers in Christ's Second Appearing," also known as "The Millennial Church." Having its beginning in a Quaker revival in England in 1747, the sect moved to America in 1774. Under the leadership of Ann Lee (whose name was shortened from Lees when she reached America), disciples were gathered in New York and in New England. In 1805 Shaker preachers were sent to Kentucky, where they acquired converts and established a temporary settlement on Shawnee Run in Mercer County near Lexington. From 1805 to 1812, the Shakers acquired 3,000 acres of land nearby, and in 1812 they established their settlement at Pleasant Hill near Harrodsburg. There they constructed some twenty brick and stone buildings. The Shaker settlement at Pleasant Hill flourished until about 1875; it commenced to decline at that time and was finally ended in 1910. The Shakers refused to accept marriage as a

Christian institution, and believed in a life of celibacy, common possession of property, nonresistance, and open confession of sins. Their common name "Shaker" was derived from their practice of accompanying their religious worship with singing and dancing and the shaking and contorting of their bodies.

7. Membership in the Shaker faith consisted solely of converts and the unmarried mothers and homeless children the Shakers took in. The Shaker edict against cohabitation of married couples resulted in no births within the society, the major reason that as of 2006 the religious group was almost extinct, with only four members remaining, all living in the Shaker community at Sabbathday Lake, Maine.

8. In the Shaker community, deacons and deaconesses had charge of temporal matters and elders and elderesses of spiritual affairs. Edward Deming Andrews, *The People Called Shakers* (New York, 1953), 255–60.

9. Shakers were organized in orders referred to as "families." The Shaker community at Pleasant Hill, which attained a maximum membership of about 500 persons, was composed of eight families. *Ibid.*, 58, 291.

10. The Millennial Laws of the Shakers provided that boys and girls "should never be schooled together." *Ibid.*, 276.

11. A physician by training, Dr. John Shain supervised the growing of the society's medicinal herbs. In his travels he collected orphans to be raised by the Society at Pleasant Hill. See Thomas D. Clark and F. Gerald Ham, *Pleasant Hill and Its Shakers* (Pleasant Hill, Kentucky, 1968), 40, 63.

12. Concerning confession of sins, the *Millennial Laws* of the Shakers provided:

    "No Believers [Shakers] can be justified in keeping any sin covered, under any pretence whatever, but all are required to make confession thereof to those who are appointed in the order of God to hear them.

    "2. If any member should know of any sin or actual transgression of the Law of Christ, in any one of the family or society, and have reason to believe the same is not known, or has not been confessed in order, the member to whom the matter is known is bound to reveal it to the Elders, so that sin may be put away, otherwise they participate in the guilt and condemnation thereof." *Ibid.*, 261.

13. The Shakers at Pleasant Hill drew up and signed a Church Covenant on June 2, 1814 that was virtually the charter of the church at Pleasant Hill. Among the original signatories of the covenant were Nelly Flemin and Maria Saylor. Daniel M. Hutton, *Old Shakertown and the Shakers*, 24.

14. Anthony Dunlavy was another of the original signatories of the Church Covenant at Pleasant Hill. *Ibid.* His brother John, also an original signatory of the Church Covenant at Pleasant Hill, wrote *The Manifesto*, an important Shaker publication representing the views of a largely self-taught biblical scholar who was able to harmonize the teachings of Shakerism with the scriptures.

15. Allen Joseph Stout was born December 5, 1815 in Danville, Mercer County, Kentucky, the tenth child of Joseph and Anna Stout. For unknown reasons, Hosea in his autobiography called his brother Joseph Allen instead of his proper name, Allen Joseph.

16. The Shakers were frequently reluctant to give up adopted children to their parents. As a result, mobs raised up against the Shaker community of Union Village in Warren County, Ohio, several times, particularly in 1819 and 1824, demanding that some children be allowed to reunite with parents. J. P. MacLean, *Shakers of Ohio*, 383–84.

17.  "All wrestling, scuffling, beating, striking, or fighting" was forbidden by the gospel of the Shakers. Deming, *People Called Shakers*, 278.

18.  Ephraim Stout, brother of Hosea Stout's father, appears to have been an adventurous and restless person who preferred not to live too close to civilization. Born February 2, 1775 in Orange County, North Carolina, he moved with his family in 1792 to eastern Tennessee and in 1801 became one of the first settlers in Wayne County, Missouri. Of him, it was written in Dr. E. Duis, *The Good Old Times in McLean County, Illinois* (Bloomington, Illinois, 1874), 217–18:

> "Ephraim Stout was a great hunter, greater than Nimrod, or Esau, or Daniel Boone, indeed the latter had been a companion to Ephraim, and many were the stories told by him of their adventures together. When Ephraim was a young man he became married, of course, but no sooner had he done so than he regretted it bitterly. He loved his wife with all the love of a young husband, but he happened to meet with Lewis and Clark, government agents, who were going to explore Oregon Territory, and his marriage prevented him from going with them. Then there was wailing and gnashing of teeth, and he declared he would give five hundred dollars to be unmarried!"

19.  Isaac Stout, an older brother of Hosea's father, Joseph, was born in North Carolina on April 14, 1768. He settled on Lytle's Creek in Clinton County after transferring his Quaker membership from Cane Creek Monthly Meeting to Center Monthly Meeting on June 4, 1808. The third schoolhouse in Clinton County was built on his farm in 1814.

20.  Hosea's uncles, Isaac and David, his Aunt Mary and Cousin John appear to have settled near Wilmington on Lytle's Creek, a stream flowing westerly from Wilmington to its junction with Todd Fork about a mile east of the westerly line of Clinton County.

21.  James McVey, an early resident of Clinton County, was born April 15, 1786 and died in Clinton County April 11, 1859, shortly before his seventy-third birthday.

22.  Jesse Stout, born February 23, 1794 in Orange County, North Carolina, was a son of Isaac Stout. Before Jesse reached his first birthday, Isaac relocated his family to Tennessee.

23.  The "distant" relationship was through the marriage of Hosea's aunt, Rachel Stout, to John Allen at Cane Creek, North Carolina. It is not known exactly how closely Joel and John were related.

24.  Lydia, born January 24, 1803 in Jefferson County, Tennessee, was Isaac Stout's daughter (not to be confused with Hosea Stout's younger sister Lydia Roena).

25.  Hiram Madden was a resident of Wilson Township, Clinton County, Ohio; his principle occupation was that of a surveyor.

26.  Elizabeth Stout was born March 5, 1822.

27.  Adam Reynard was born in Germany in about 1764. According to Hosea Stout, he was a distant relative. On June 13, 1834, Adam Reynard Jr. married Isaac Stout's daughter, Mary. This marriage may be the reason Hosea Stout described Adam Reynard as a distant relative at the time he wrote his autobiography in the winter of 1846–47.

28.  This is a reference to Job Simcock, born April 12, 1803. According to Quaker records at Springfield Monthly Meeting, Simcock arrived in Clinton County in 1823 and in 1825 married Catherine Reynard, daughter of Adam Reynard Sr. Being only seven

years senior to Hosea, the nickname "Grand-Dadda" obviously was not in reference to Simcock's age.

29. Allen Stout in his journal referred to him as William McStout. See Journal of Allen Joseph Stout.

30. Applejack or "cider oil," as it was once known, is made in colder climates simply by allowing hard cider to freeze and then removing the ice, thereby increasing the strength of the remaining liquid.

31. In the early nineteenth century, rubella was thought to be halfway between measles and scarlet fever. French scientists made important contributions to the study of the disease, leading to the name French measles, but since German scientists did most of the work, the disease later became known as the German measles.

32. Spotted measles later became known simply as measles, or rubeola. The name was derived from the fact that in early stages of the disease, what later becomes a full body rash begins as spots on the forehead, then spreads downward over the face, neck, and body, then down to the feet.

33. Samuel Stout, born April 14, 1771 in Orange County, North Carolina, was an older brother of Hosea's father. He settled in Tennessee in 1792 and thereafter, in about 1827, moved to Tazewell County, Illinois, being the first settler in a community called Little Mackinaw.

34. Benjamin Howell, born July 14, 1792, emigrated to Ohio with his father and eight siblings prior to 1810. By 1823 all of the family save Benjamin had moved farther west. His brother Charles was married to Hosea's second cousin, Mary Stout.

35. John Fallis was born in 1754 in Falmouth County, Virginia. His Quaker membership was transferred on May 2, 1796 to the Redstone (Pennsylvania) Monthly Meeting, which had jurisdiction over the newly settled Quaker colony in Clinton County, Ohio. He was disowned by the Quakers in 1828 for "disunity."

36. Eli Harvey was born in North Carolina on March 9, 1803. His parents, William and Mary Harvey, migrated in 1807 to Clinton County from North Carolina, where they, along with Hosea Stout's parents, grandparents, and great-grandparents, were members of Cane Creek Monthly Meeting. Eli married Sarah Fallis, daughter of John Fallis, on March 27, 1824. A grandson of the same name became an internationally known artist and sculptor. Hosea held Eli in such high regard that he named a son, born September 17, 1851 in Salt Lake City, Eli Harvey Stout.

37. Isaiah Morris, a native of Pennsylvania, moved to Ohio in 1803 and was one of the earliest settlers in Wilmington. From 1817 to 1837 he served as clerk of the Supreme Court in Clinton County.

38. Andrew Jackson had 41.3 percent of the popular vote and 99 electoral votes compared to 30.9 percent of the popular vote and 84 electoral votes for John Quincy Adams; William Harris Crawford had 41 electoral votes and Henry Clay 37. As no candidate received more than 50 percent of the electoral votes, under the provisions of Twelfth Amendment to the Constitution, the House of Representatives voted to decide the election. Clay did not believe that Jackson's success as a general meant he was ready for the presidency and thus supported Adams, who with Clay's support won the election and later selected Clay to be his Secretary of State, thus opening the way for charges that it was a "corrupt bargain."

39. Hosea was fourteen years old at this time.

40. In the fall of 1824, Hosea's father, Joseph Stout, with his daughters, Mary, Anna, and Lydia, and his son, Allen Joseph, moved to Cincinnati. After remaining there a few

weeks, they moved to the falls of the Ohio River, near Louisville, where they spent the winter. There Mary married Nicholas Jameson. In the spring of 1825, Hosea's father, leaving his daughter, Lydia, with Mary, but accompanied by Anna and Allen Joseph, set out by river boat for Little Rock, Arkansas. On the way he had a falling out with the boat captain, so went ashore before reaching Little Rock. Eventually, he joined his brother, Ephraim, in Washington County, Missouri, and moved with him to Tazewell County, Illinois. In 1827 he left Anna and Allen Joseph in Illinois and returned to Ohio. A full account of these events is contained in the Journal of Allen Joseph Stout, typescripts in the library of the Utah State Historical Society and in the Henry E. Huntington Library and Art Gallery, at San Marino, California.

41. Ezekiel Hornaday was born in North Carolina February 26, 1796 and came to Ohio in 1807 with the Harvey brothers (Eli's father William and uncle Isaac) and their families. Having been left an orphan at an early age, he was bound out to Isaac Harvey, in whose family he was raised. Jesse Harvey, a son of Isaac, was Eli Harvey's cousin.

42. George Carter began teaching in Clinton County as early as 1812 or 1813. It was about a year later that neighbors built a log schoolhouse on the Carter's farm. He taught in that schoolhouse for several terms, and afterward at Lytle's Creek and various other places in the county.

43. *Kirkham's Grammar* is a comprehensive 228-page compendium of the rules of English grammar. It was published in the first decades of the nineteenth century "for the use of schools and private learners." *Kirkham's Grammar* was ordinarily the second book, after the Bible, in the collection of every frontier library.

44. Stephen Stout was born September 29, 1802 in North Carolina, where his parents were members of Cane Creek Monthly Meeting. His grandfather, Charles Stout, was a younger brother of Hosea's grandfather Samuel.

45. Todd's Fork begins northeast of Wilmington and flows in a generally southwesterly direction through Clinton and Warren counties, Ohio, to its juncture with the Little Miami River.

46. Mackinaw, Illinois, is about twenty miles west of Bloomington and about the same distance southeast of Peoria. In 1828 Mackinaw was the county seat of Tazewell County, but in 1831 the county seat was moved to Pekin.

47. In the early 1800s, large quantities of lead and zinc were mined in the extreme northwestern part of Illinois, around the city of Galena.

48. The name Grassy Run is taken from that of a small tributary of Anderson's Fork in Wilson Township and extending across the county line into Montgomery County. It was site of the Quakers' Grassy Run Monthly Meeting.

49. In 1806 Congress granted an appropriation for the building of a highway leading west through the Appalachians, which came to be known as the National Road. It began at Cumberland, Maryland, and by 1820 had progressed as far as Wheeling, Ohio. From Wheeling, travel could continue by river boat. Nonetheless, the building of the highway continued toward St. Louis, but in 1836 it was discontinued after reaching Vandalia, Illinois. A. B. Hulbert, *Paths of Inland Commerce* (New Haven, 1920), *passim*.

50. Spicewood is a shrub whose bark has a spicy taste and odor. It is also commonly called wild allspice.

51. Hosea's uncle, Ephraim Stout, is referred to in Duis, *The Good Old Times in McLean County*, 217, as the most eccentric man in the area. However, he is described somewhat more kindly in *The History of McLean County, Illinois* (Chicago, 1879), 567, which says of him as follows:

    "Ephraim Stout was a large man of commanding presence. His early education had been neglected, so that he could not be said to have much book knowledge; but his practical knowledge of the world was extensive, and his ability to judge the qualities of men almost complete. He and all those immediately connected with him were Friends [Quakers]. This man had a son named Ephraim, who was married and came to the Grove with his father. They lived at the Grove a long time, and then moved farther west, finally settling in Oregon."

52. Stout's Grove was located six or seven miles east of Mackinaw and occupied much of what is now Danvers Township in the northwestern part of McLean County, Illinois. Prior to 1831 it was in Tazewell County. A map published by Peter Folsom, county surveyor of McLean County in 1856, showed Stout's Grove as containing 11,200 acres.

    In 1825 Hosea Stout's uncle, Ephraim Stout, and cousin, Ephraim Jr., and their families with Ephraim's nephew, Amasa Stout, moved from Washington County, Missouri, to Tazewell County, Illinois, and settled at the southeast corner of Stout's Grove about twelve miles west of Bloomington and about one mile west of the present town of Danvers, Illinois. There they established the settlement of Stout's Grove. According to the journal of Hosea Stout's younger brother, Allen Joseph, he (Allen), Anna, their father, and also their paternal grandmother accompanied Ephraim Stout on his move from Missouri to Stout's Grove. Hosea's father, Joseph, did not remain very long but moved on to Galena in northwestern Illinois and finally returned to Ohio, leaving Allen Joseph and Anna at Dillon's Settlement. *Historical Encyclopedia of Illinois and History of McLean County* (Chicago, 1908), I, 626.

53. Amasa Stout, Hosea's cousin, was born in 1799 in Guilford County, North Carolina, a son of Joseph Stout's oldest brother Peter.

54. Dillon Settlement, about twenty miles southwest of Stout's Grove, was settled in 1823 by Nathan Dillon, reputedly the first settler in Tazewell County, Illinois.

55. Barrens are level tracts of land poorly forested and commonly having light sandy soil, such as pine barrens and oak barrens.

56. Little Mackinaw Grove, about seven miles southwest of Mackinaw, Illinois, on the Little Mackinaw River, was first settled by Samuel and John Stout. Samuel was Joseph Stout's brother; John, born in Orange County, North Carolina on August 8, 1789, was Amasa Stout's brother. On June 24, 1827, John married his cousin Fannie, Samuel Stout's daughter, in the first marriage performed after the organization of Tazewell County. He would appear to be the "Big John" hereafter referred to by Hosea. *History of Tazewell County* (Chicago, 1879), 211–12.

57. Daniel Hodgson was born to Quaker parents in Guilford County, North Carolina June 12, 1784. His daughter, Ann, married Martin Myers in Clinton County, Ohio, on August 4, 1825.

58. Jonas Hittle was born March 21, 1806 in Greene County, Ohio, and is reported to have been the first justice of the peace in Tazewell County. On March 3, 1828 he applied to the county commissioners' court of Tazewell County for a license to operate a tavern. This was granted, but the license restricted the rates he could

charge to 6 ¼ cents per person for lodging and 18 ¾ cents for each meal. *History of Tazewell County,* 234.

59.   Brown's Grove comprised some 560 acres. It was named for the Reverend William Brown, referred to as "Preacher" Brown, who moved there from Tennessee in 1826, but thereafter moved to Mackinaw. The marriage of Amasa Stout and Susan Smith was performed by him October 15, 1828. Mrs. George Spangler, "Early Marriages in Tazewell County," *Journal of the Illinois State Historical Society,* XIV (April, 1931), 145.

60.   "Infair" is a Scottish and regional American term applied to a celebration in connection with a wedding, installation of a new minister, or other special event.

61.   Dr. Griffith was a Quaker physician who practiced medicine in Pekin at the time of an epidemic of Asiatic Cholera in Tazewell County in the summer of 1834. Of him it was written: "This was the act of the good old Quaker friend, Dr. Griffith. Personal test compels the declaration that his doses of 'Peruvian barks' for 'fever 'n ager' were large, frequent and very bitter, but his words, when he said: 'James, these will make thee better,' were sweet as the fabled honey of Hymettus, and his gentle hand when he pressed the fevered brow was soft and cool as the leaves that fall in Vallombrosa's Vale." See *Transactions of the Illinois State Historical Society,* 1905.

62.   Hosea Stout's three uncles living in Tazewell County were his father's brothers, Ephraim living at Stout's Grove, David who had settled at Brown's Grove, and Samuel living at Little Mackinaw Grove. The aunt referred to as living on Little Mackinaw was probably his father's sister, Rachel. Hosea's paternal grandmother, Rachel Chancy Stout, at this time was 87 years of age, and his aunt, Margaret, sister of his father, was 63 years of age. Rachel Chancy Stout died in 1831.

63.   Jesse Stout, son of Hosea's uncle, Isaac, had recently moved to Tazewell County, Illinois, from Clinton County, Ohio, where he had previously taught Hosea in school.

64.   Of Ephraim Stout and his opposition to all except the Quaker religion, it is stated in Duis, *The Good Old Times in McLean County,* 218–19:

"Ephraim Stout was a Quaker, and when he settled in Stout's Grove he thought he would make of it a Quaker settlement. He collected Quakers from far and near and everything seemed 'merry as a marriage bell'; but in an evil hour he allowed Squire Robb, who was a Cumberland Presbyterian, to come in to the settlement. Now Squire Robb had married a daughter of a gentleman named McClure [in August of 1821, Matthew Robb married Mary McClure, daughter of Thomas McClure], and when the former settled in Stout's Grove the McClure family insisted on settling there too, and they were followed by some one else, and these by still others until that Quaker settlement was swallowed up, and the soul of poor old Ephraim Stout was racked within him. He was accustomed to live in the wild woods, and did not like to see so many people around him. When he was married he had promised his wife that he would always live in the forest *where she could pick her own fire-wood,* and when so many people came there and broke up his Quaker settlement, he picked up his gun and all his hunter's accoutrements and started for Iowa Territory and then for Oregon. In 1830 he was an old man, leaning on his staff for support, and when he told the stories of his adventures with Indians and with all the wild animals of the forest, it certainly seemed that it was time for him to rest from his labors and live the remainder of his life in peace; but there was no peace for him within the bounds of civilization, so he gathered together his worldly goods and went out to the still farther West."

65. Cumberland Presbyterians separated from the Presbyterian Church in 1802 in southern Kentucky and Tennessee, for the purpose of licensing and ordaining men who could not meet the educational qualifications established by the old Presbytery. This step was considered justified to meet the increased demand for preachers brought about by the religious revival on the frontier at the beginning of the nineteenth century.

66. According to Owenetta Edwards, "Early Schools and Teachers in my County," *Journal of the Illinois State Historical Society*, XXIV (April, 1931), 14, "Archibald Johnson, who taught a subscription school about the winter of 1832–3 was the first teacher in Danvers [Illinois]. He was a Cumberland preacher and a good teacher. His price per scholar for a term of four months was $2.00. The second teacher was Lyman Porter; and the third was Hosea Stout, who was converted to Mormonism. He went to Nauvoo and afterwards to Salt Lake City, where he became one of the twelve apostles." The statement that Hosea Stout became one the Twelve Apostles of the Mormon Church is incorrect.

67. Funk's Grove was named for Isaac Funk and his brother, Abraham, who settled there in 1824. The Grove comprised approximately 2,700 acres according to a survey map published by Peter Folsom, county surveyor of McLean County in 1856, and consisted of sugar and black maples.

68. Blooming Grove is now a part of the present city of Bloomington, Illinois, the county seat of McLean County. It was originally settled in 1822 as Keg Grove.

69. Pekin, Illinois, is located on the east side of the Illinois River about five miles south of Peoria and about fifteen miles west of Mackinaw. In 1831 it became the county seat of Tazewell County.

70. Morris Phelps settled in Tazewell County a few miles west of Pekin shortly after his marriage in 1826. Soon after Hosea Stout ceased working for him, Phelps moved to the northern part of Illinois, where he became a convert to Mormonism. After being baptized in August of 1831, he sold his possessions in Illinois and started for Jackson County, Missouri, to join the members of the church there. He and other members were driven successively from Jackson County and from Caldwell County, Missouri, and Nauvoo, Illinois, and he finally settled in Utah, where he died May 22, 1876.

71. Farm Creek flows in a westerly direction through the northern portion of Tazewell County from near the town of Washington to its terminus at the Illinois River at the southern end of Lake Peoria.

72. Charles Coulson Rich, born August 21, 1809 in northwestern Kentucky, was a lifelong friend and associate of Hosea Stout; one of Rich's plural wives, Sarah Peck, was the sister of Stout's first wife Samantha. One of the earlier Illinois converts to Mormonism (in 1832), Rich in 1836 led fellow converts in Tazewell County to Caldwell County, Missouri, to join the Saints who gathered there. Rich was very influential in Stout's conversion and move to Caldwell County.

   After the Saints were expelled from Missouri in 1838 and 1839, and established their city of Nauvoo in Hancock County, Illinois, Rich became a member of the city council and also of the High Council of the church there, and rose to high rank in the Nauvoo Legion, the military arm of the Mormons. In 1849 he was ordained a member of the Quorum of Twelve Apostles of the Church of Jesus Christ of Latter-day Saints. He cofounded the city of San Bernardino, California, with Amasa M. Lyman, a fellow apostle in the church.

73. Like his brother, Neil Johnson was a Cumberland Presbyterian minister. The first twenty years of his work in the ministry were spent in Illinois and Iowa, after which, in 1851, he moved to Oregon with his wife and nine children.

74. Named after George Rogers Clark, a Revolutionary War hero at Vincennes in 1778, the fort was erected by militia forces in 1813 and partially destroyed by fire in 1818. It was rebuilt in 1832 in response to the Black Hawk War.

75. In *History of Tazewell County*, 331, the malady that appears to have stricken Hosea Stout is described as follows:

    "One of the greatest obstacles, and one which wielded a very potent influence in retarding the early settlement of this county, was the 'chills and fever', or the 'ague', or the 'Illinois shakes', as it was variously styled. This disease was a terror to new comers. In the fall of the year everybody was afflicted with it. It was no respecter of persons; everyone shook with it, and it was in every person's system. They all looked pale and yellow as though they were frostbitten. It was not contagious, but was a kind of miasma that floated around in the atmosphere and was absorbed into the system. It continued to be absorbed from day to day, and week to week, until the whole body corporate became charged with it as with electricity, and then the shock came, and the shock was a regular shake, with a fixed beginning and an ending, coming on each day, or each alternate day, with a regularity that was surprising. After the shake came the fever, and this 'last estate was worse than the first'. It was a burning hot fever and lasted for hours. When you had the chill you couldn't get warm, and when you had the fever you couldn't get cool."

76. Matthew Robb was the first justice of the peace in Stout's Grove, elected in 1827 and holding the office for twelve years.

77. Sanford Porter was born March 7, 1790, in Brimfield, Massachusetts. An early convert to Mormonism (in 1831), Porter that same year baptized his neighbor, Morris Phelps. In 1846 he was a member of the Mormon Battalion and was a 1847 Utah pioneer, having reached the Salt Lake Valley from California following his service in the Battalion.

78. William Eads, together with William Davis, is reputed to have constructed the first grist mill in Tazewell County in 1825 near Pekin. Later on, Eads built a cotton gin in connection with the grist mill.

79. In *History of Tazewell County*, 214–15, the winter of 1830 is described as follows: "The big snow of 1830 will be remembered by all the old settlers. The snow began falling on the night of the 29th of December, and continued to fall for three days and nights, until it reached an average depth of about four feet, but drifting in places as high as eighteen to twenty feet. Great suffering was experienced in consequence." Storms with high winds continued throughout the state for 60 days. It is still known as the "Winter of the Deep Snow."

80. Lyman Porter succeeded Archibald Johnson as schoolmaster at Stout's Grove. Born in Vermont in 1804, Porter also ran a store in Mackinaw.

81. Hosea Stout's father and brother, Allen Joseph, journeyed down the Illinois River with the purpose of going to Texas. When within seven miles of the Texas border, they learned they could continue no further because of the outbreak of fighting between the Texans and Mexicans, they settled in southern Arkansas, where they remained until 1837. Journal of Allen Joseph Stout.

82. Later promoted to colonel, Robert McClure served as a captain in Major Stillman's battalion, Whiteside's Brigade, in the Black Hawk War of 1832.

83. Benjamin Conger is listed as having served along with Robert McClure in Whiteside's Brigade in the Black Hawk War. The Conger family settled at Stout's Grove in 1829.

84. Walnut Grove was situated on Walnut Creek in Tazewell County, near the present-day town of Eureka, Illinois.

85. The Ox-Bow Prairie is the name given an irregularly shaped farming region about five miles in length from east to west and varying from one to two and a half miles in width from north to south. Shaped like an oxbow, surrounded by timber and formerly a part of Putnam County, the Ox-Bow Prairie was a part of the territory cut off from that county in 1835 to form Marshall County, Illinois. Asahel Hannum was one of the first settlers in the Ox-Bow Prairie.

86. The Black Hawk War arose out of the refusal of a band of Sauk Indians under the leadership of their chief, Black Hawk, to move to a reservation west of the Mississippi River. After defeating a force under Major Isaiah Stillman that had been sent after them, the Indians began depredations upon white settlements. A call was made for volunteers, and several companies of militia were organized as a precautionary measure along the east bank of the Illinois River. One such company was the 40th Regiment, Illinois Militia, commanded by Colonel John Strawn. On May 21, 1832, Hosea Stout volunteered for service in the 40th Regiment and served in William Haws's company. The regiment was assigned to patrol along the Illinois River. As soon as it was determined there was no danger from the Indians in the vicinity, and following the defeat of Black Hawk in the Battle of Bad Axe, the members of the regiment were mustered out of service at Hennepin, Illinois, June 18, 1832. John Spencer Burt and W. E. Hawthorne, *Past and Present of Marshall and Putnam Counties, Illinois* (Chicago, 1907), 23; and Perry A. Armstrong, *The Sauks and the Black Hawk War* (Springfield, 1887), 684.

87. One of the depredations by the Indians during the Black Hawk War was upon a little settlement on Indian Creek where the Davis, Hall, and Pettigrew families lived. After massacring the families, the Indians discovered two survivors, Rachel and Sylvia Hall, age fifteen and seventeen, who had escaped by concealing themselves. The Hall sisters were taken captive, but were eventually ransomed. *History of Tazewell County*, 261–62.

88. Hosea Stout appears to be mistaken when he states the Hall sisters married the Muson brothers. According to Spencer Ellsworth, *Records of the Olden Times; or Fifty Years on the Prairies* (Lacon, Illinois, 1880), 118, Rachel Hall married William Munson and Sylvia Hall married William Horn.

89. Benjamin Jones was born February 24, 1797 in Chehoching, New York. Anna Stout married Jones November 29, 1832 in a ceremony performed by Charles Coulson Rich. Spangler, "Early Marriages in Tazewell County," *Journal of the Illinois State Historical Society*, XIV, 145.

90. Joseph Smith, the founder of the Church of Jesus Christ of Latter-day Saints (more popularly known as the Mormon Church), claimed a heavenly being gave him information concerning records of the ancient inhabitants of America, written on plates of gold, and buried near Palmyra, New York. He translated the records, which were published as the Book of Mormon. In 1830 he established a church and in 1831 settled with a number of his adherents at Kirtland, Ohio, near the present city of Cleveland. Other of his followers established a branch of the church at Independence, Jackson County, Missouri. Opposition to the Mormons in Jackson County

led to open hostilities against them during most of the year 1833, and at the end of the year they were expelled from Jackson County, many of them thereafter moving north to Clay and other adjoining counties in Missouri.

91. Nathan Wixom was born November 22, 1804 in Hector Township, Schuyler, New York, and lived in Troy Grove, Tazewell County.

92. According to Duis, *The Good Old Times in McLean County*, 217, the school taught by Hosea Stout "was attended by thirty or forty children, who came great distances and boarded with the farmers near by."

93. Crow Creek rises in the north part of McLean County, passes through the southwestern part of La Salle and enters the Illinois river in Putnam county below Hennepin. It is bordered both by good timber and fertile soil.

94. The sawmill on Farm Creek purchased from Nathan Wixom by Hosea Stout and Benjamin Jones was located three miles east of Peoria.

95. On November 13, 1833, residents of the eastern United States were awakened to what appeared to be the heavens descending. In the early morning hours up to 150,000 shooting stars were seen descending from the skies. Frightened people gathered in the streets and many wondered what had angered their gods. Following this event, all sorts of religious revivals were triggered around the world. On that night, the Mormons were being expelled from Jackson County, Missouri, and regarded the meteor shower as a heavenly manifestation connected with their expulsion.

96. Six months following the Mormon expulsion from Jackson County, a force of about 150 men was gathered at Kirtland, Ohio, to march to Missouri and "redeem Zion," primarily by restoring confiscated land to its rightful Mormon owner. Upon arrival in Missouri, the hostility of the people there made it evident that the "redemption of Zion" would have to await some other opportunity. The force, which had increased to about 200 and was known as Zion's Camp, was disbanded a day after cholera broke out in the camp, which resulted in the death of thirteen of its members.

97. Hyrum Smith, born February 9, 1800 at Tunbridge, Vermont, was an older brother of Joseph Smith. From 1837 until 1841 he served as counselor to Joseph Smith, president of the church. In 1841 Hyrum assumed the office of Patriarch to the Church, which he held until he and Joseph were assassinated by a mob on June 27, 1844 at Carthage, Illinois.

98. Lyman Wight, born May 9, 1796 at Fairfield, New York, was one of the prophet's most ardent early followers; he was appointed an apostle in the church in 1841. Following the assassination of Joseph and Hyrum Smith in 1844, Wight refused to acknowledge the authority of the Quorum of Twelve Apostles under Brigham Young as successor to the prophet and was excommunicated in 1848. He led a body of adherents to Texas, where he died in 1858.

99. This may have been the same lawsuit referred to in Ellsworth, *Records of the Olden Time*, 359: "In 1834 Joe Martin put up a mill on Crow Creek, about forty rods below Owens' Mill, but his dam backed water upon the latter, and he could get no sufficient head. A lawsuit grew out of this affair, and Martin finally abandoned his mill project here and went farther down the stream, where he began again on a sawmill, but shortly afterward sold to Samuel Headlock."

100. This entry concludes the first portion of the autobiography. The second autobiography is shorter, more concise, and less illuminating. It covers the whole period

of Hosea Stout's life up to 1844. There is an overlapping of the years 1810 to 1835, already covered in this first portion of the autobiography.

## The Autobiography of Hosea Stout, 1810 to 1844

101. In 1845 Hosea Stout wrote the following autobiographical sketch for the records of the Eleventh Quorum of Seventies in Nauvoo, Illinois. This composition is of interest because it is concerned principally with the period from 1835 to 1844, a period not covered in his previous autobiography.

102. Concerning Hosea's activities while living in Wesley City, Tazewell County, Illinois, and the migration of the Mormons living there to Caldwell County, Missouri, in 1837, Allen Stout, Hosea's brother who returned to Tazawell County with his father from Arkansas after an absence of six years, wrote in his journal:

"Benjamin Jones who had married my sister Anna kept a boarding house [in Wesley City], and he and Hosea were at carpenter work with them, and at evenings I read the book of Doctrine and Covenants [a book of divine revelations considered by Mormons to have been given their prophet, Joseph Smith]; I could not get hold of a Book of Mormon. I went to a number of Sunday prayer meetings but still the most satisfaction I could get was what Hosea would tell me for he was as well acquainted with the Gospel as he is now, but had not obeyed it yet. Soon after we got here Lyman Wight, Charles C. Rich and Morris Phelps came on from Missouri and held a meeting, so we all went to hear, and I was well pleased, and so was father, but to my great astonishment, some were very mad and said they did not teach the Scriptures. But I knew better for I was well acquainted with the Bible.

"On the 5th of July, 1837, Father and I set out for Caldwell County, Missouri, in company with Anna and Jones' family, and what was called the 'Rich' branch of the Church. C. C. Rich was our leader. Hosea, Benjamin [Jones] and Lydia staid behind to finish some jobs and settle some business, and then came on by water. We crossed the Mississippi at Quincy and traveled through Palmyra, Huntsville, Keetsville, and Carlton. We got to our journey's end about the 6th of August. My business on the road was to drive sheep and help Anna about the camping business....Hosea and Ben soon came on and Hosea had a good bag of cash, so he entered 200 acres of good land, and we went to work and built a house on it, and Lydia kept house for us...." Journal of Allen Stout, 6–7.

103. Following their expulsion from Jackson County, Missouri, in 1833, and after a temporary stay in Clay County, the Mormons settled in 1836 in Caldwell County, Missouri, where they established their communities of Far West and Adam-ondi-Ahman. These settlements grew rapidly as Mormons poured into Caldwell and adjacent counties, most of them in small groups, but many in large companies such as the expedition of over one hundred families comprising Kirtland Camp that journeyed in a body from Kirtland, Ohio, to Far West and Adam-ondi-Ahman in 1838. On August 6, 1838, hostilities between the Mormons and their neighbors broke out following an attempt to prevent the Mormons from voting. Both sides promptly took up arms against the other. Eventually the Mormons capitulated and were driven from the state of Missouri, from where they settled in Hancock County, Illinois, and established their city of Nauvoo.

104. David W. Patten was a member of the Council of Twelve Apostles of the Mormon Church from 1835, when the council was first organized, until his death.

105. On the night of October 24, 1838, Captain Bogart's company went to the home of Nathan Pinkham and took Pinkham, William Seeley, and Addison Green, all Mormons, prisoner.

106. The comment that "many a mobber was there baptised without faith or repentance" refers to the Mormon belief that baptism must be accompanied by faith in Jesus Christ and repentance to effect salvation. The summons to appear and give an account of one's stewardship has reference to the appearance all are considered required to make before the Judgment Bar following death. And the observation that those killed by the Mormons in the Battle of Crooked River lost their lives "in an attempt to murder those who will Judge them at the Great day" arises out of the statement in Section 75 of the *Doctrine and Covenants*, which instructed the Mormon elders to carry the gospel from house-to-house, declaring "And in whatsoever house ye enter, and they receive you not, ye shall depart speedily from that house, and shake off the dust of your feet as a testimony against them. And you shall be filled with joy and gladness; and know this, that in the day of judgment you shall be judges of that house, and condemn them; And it shall be more tolerable for the heathen in the day of judgment, than for that house;..." This is interpreted by reference to John 5:20 and Matthew 19:28 as meaning that Christ, to whom God "hath committed all judgment," would sit in judgment upon all men, but that the elders would assist in the judgment of and would give testimony against, those who were offered but refused to receive the gospel.

107. All of the named wounded recovered with the exception James Hendrix, who was crippled for the remainder of his life.

108. Stephen Winchester acted as captain of a company in the march of Zion's Camp from Kirtland, Ohio, to Missouri in 1834. Thereafter he returned to Kirtland, but in 1837, he settled south of Far West, where he lived until the Saints were driven out of Missouri into Illinois. In 1846, he left Nauvoo, and after remaining at Winter Quarters until 1849, he moved to Salt Lake City, where he died in 1873.

109. Hosea's report of the losses suffered by Bogart's company is greatly exaggerated. The number of casualties Bogart's force suffered is given as one killed and six wounded in *History of Caldwell and Livingston Counties* (St. Louis, 1886), 129–30. Stout's estimate, however, is not so exaggerated as the report given by members of Bogart's company that Bogart's command had been attacked by three hundred Mormons, and that the Mormons had killed ten, many others had been wounded, and most of the remainder had been taken prisoner. Report also was made to Governor Lilburn W. Boggs that all of Bogart's command except three men had been massacred.

110. On the basis of reports of the Battle of Crooked River and other reports of violence, Governor Lilburn W. Boggs issued an order to the state militia that "The Mormons must be treated as enemies, and must be exterminated or driven from the state if necessary for the public peace." Twenty-five hundred men were raised by order of Governor Boggs to carry the order into effect. Orders to raise additional forces do not appear to have been carried out.

111. On October 31, 1838, the Mormons at Far West were preparing for battle with a force of some 2,200 to 3,000 men raised to carry Governor Boggs's extermination order into effect. Under a flag of truce, Colonel George M. Hinkle and John Corrill representing the Mormons met certain officers of the militia forces and secretly

entered into an agreement to surrender and to give up the leaders of the church. Upon their return to Far West, Hinkle reported that the chief officers of the militia desired an interview with Joseph Smith and his counselor, Sidney Rigdon; apostles Parley P. Pratt and Lyman Wight; and church recorder George W. Robinson, all of whom accompanied Hinkle back to the militia camp, where to their surprise they were delivered to the militia forces as prisoners of war. Hinkle, Corrill, Reed Peck, and others testified against the Mormon leaders so captured. Rollin J. Britton, "Early Days on Grand River and the Mormon War," *Missouri Historical Review*, XIII, 306–7; B. H. Roberts, *A Comprehensive History of the Church of Jesus Christ of Latter-day Saints* (Salt Lake City, 1930), I, 485–87.

112. Besides Hosea, the twenty-seven who made their escape included Charles C. Rich, Lorenzo Dow Young and Phineas H. Young (brothers of Brigham Young), Samuel H. Smith (a brother of the Mormon prophet), Benjamin L. Clapp, Robert B. Thompson, Isaac Higbee, and Titus Billings. The flight of the twenty-seven from Missouri to avoid prosecution for murder because of their participation in the Battle of Crooked River was counseled by Brigham Young. General John B. Clark of the Missouri State Militia is reported to have dispatched a company of fifty armed men to follow and arrest them. Messengers were sent from Far West to report this to the fugitives, who upon learning they were being pursued vowed to fight if overtaken. After traveling about ten miles farther, the twenty-seven camped on the edge of some timber on the north side of a prairie. Their pursuers are reputed to have camped on the south side of the prairie only four miles away. During the night a heavy snow fell. According to Mormon accounts, this storm was sent by the Lord so the militia forces could not follow the tracks of the fugitives. The militia company being unable to follow, abandoned the pursuit and reported to their general that they were unable to overtake the Mormons because of the snow storm. Andrew Jenson, *The Historical Record a Monthly Periodical* (Salt Lake City, 1889), VII, 618–19.

113. Following the surrender of the church leaders by the treachery of Hinkle, other Mormons were captured and imprisoned. Most of those charged with crimes were tried and acquitted, and others escaped. In April 1839, Joseph Smith and others imprisoned with him made their escape, apparently with the connivance of their guards. Meanwhile, most of the members of the church in Missouri left the state and moved eastward into Illinois.

114. According to Allen Stout, he sold the crop raised on Hosea Stout's two-hundred-acre farm in Caldwell County "for 75 cents per barrel and got $20 which enabled Samantha [Hosea's wife] to get to Quincy, Illinois, where she found Hosea. I then began to try to get Father and myself away for we were all forced to leave the State by the next spring…Then I took Jones' team and joined with Brother…Judd family and my father, and went to Quincy, Illinois. I found my brother [Hosea] living near that city, and I left Father there.…" Journal of Allen Joseph Stout, 9–10.

115. Of his and Hosea Stout's residence in Payson, Illinois, and Lee County, Iowa, and their move to Nauvoo, the city the Mormons established in Hancock County, Illinois, following their expulsion from Missouri, Allen Stout wrote, "…I then went out 14 miles [from Quincy] to a little town called Payson and worked with my brother [Hosea] at carpenter and other work till the 5th of July, 1839, when Hosea, Thomas Rich [a cousin of Charles C. Rich who married Henrietta Peck, a sister of Hosea's wife] and Myself started for Commerce, afterwards called Nauvoo, and came here and stayed a few days and then went over the Mississippi River into

Iowa, and then began to improve a place; and Hosea and Thomas returned back to Payson, while I stayed and worked on the house but my health was so poor that I could do but little now. Father and sister Sarah who had lately come from Ohio, left and went towards Missouri, but Sarah Died 25 miles below Quincy, of consumption; and Father went to uncle Jacob Stout's in [Washington County] Missouri, and died there, also of consumption. He was about 73 years of age; and of [his] 12 children only four [Anna, Hosea, Allen, and Lydia] was left alive. During the remainder of the summer I worked at building a house for us to live in. I also made some rails to get me some clothing....

"On the 29th of November [1839], Samantha, my brother's wife died.

"I then went back to Caldwell County, Missouri, and made a visit to see my sister Lydia [now married to John Larkey], and then returned to Iowa and spent the winter at work, sometimes making rails and some of the time building houses. In the spring of 1840 we all moved over to Nauvoo,..." Journal of Allen Joseph Stout, 10.

116. An "elder" is a member of one of the orders of the priesthood in the Mormon Church. Hosea Stout's ordination to the office of elder "under the hands" of Seymour Brunson refers to the Mormon practice of placing hands upon the head of one while he is being ordained to office or position in the church, or is receiving a blessing.

117. Pursuant to revelation announced by Joseph Smith in April 1830, general conferences are held from time-to-time by the membership of the Mormon Church to carry out whatever church business may need to be done. The first general conference was held June 9, 1830. General conferences of the church are generally held in April and October of each year.

118. Seymour Brunson was one of the early converts to the Mormon faith and was active as a missionary following his baptism in January 1831. In the spring of 1837 he settled near Far West in Caldwell County, Missouri. After being expelled from Missouri he eventually moved to Nauvoo, where he served as a member of the High Council of the church from its organization in Nauvoo in October 1839, until his death August 10, 1840.

119. The first High Council of the church was established by Joseph Smith in Kirtland, Ohio, February 12, 1834, with both judicial and administrative functions in the affairs of the church and its members. Thereafter a second High Council was formed July 3, 1834, in Missouri. As the church has grown and expanded, high councils have been organized in each ecclesiastical unit, called "stakes," of the church. In 1839 a stake was organized in both Nauvoo and in Iowa across the Mississippi River from Nauvoo, and a High Council was appointed for each. In addition to having a High Council, each stake is headed by a president having two counselors. A stake comprises a group of parishes, referred to as "wards."

120. Section 25 of the Act to Incorporate the City of Nauvoo, enacted by the Illinois Legislature in December 1840, authorized the city council to "organize the inhabitants of said city, subject to military duty, into a body of independent military men, to be called the 'Nauvoo Legion'...at the disposal of the Mayor in executing the laws and ordinances of the city corporation, and the laws of the State, and at the disposal of the Governor for the public defense, and the execution of the laws of the State or of the United States."

Pursuant to such authorization, the city council of Nauvoo passed an ordinance February 8, 1841, organizing the Nauvoo Legion. The Legion eventually numbered some four thousand men and was reputed to be the largest military organization in the United States excepting only the regular army. The Legion was divided into two cohorts and then into regiments, battalions, and companies. The first cohort comprised the horse or mounted troops, and the foot troops constituted the second cohort. Upon organization of the Legion, Joseph Smith, with the rank of lieutenant general, became its commander-in-chief, with John C. Bennett, who had been quartermaster general of the state of Illinois, the Legion's second-in-command. Wilson Law and Don Carlos Smith were placed in command of the first and second cohorts, respectively. Hamilton Gardner, "The Nauvoo Legion, 1840–1845—A Unique Military Organization," *Journal of the Illinois State Historical Society*, LIV (Summer, 1961), 181–97.

121. John Cook Bennett, referred to by Governor Thomas Ford, of Illinois, in his *History of Illinois* (New York, 1854), 263, as "probably the greatest scamp in the western country," joined the Mormon Church soon after the Saints moved to Nauvoo. He was showered by the Saints with honor after honor, being elected mayor of Nauvoo, brigadier general of the Nauvoo Legion, and to other offices. In 1843 he turned against the church and made many charges against Joseph Smith. For this Bennett was excommunicated and, thereafter, was one of the bitterest opponents of the church.

122. William Law joined the Saints at Nauvoo in the latter part of 1839. On January 19, 1841, he was appointed counselor to Joseph Smith in the presidency of the church. In 1844 he turned against Joseph Smith and was excommunicated from the church and also court martialed from the Nauvoo Legion, with Hosea serving as a member of the court martial. He was one of the publishers of the *Nauvoo Expositor*.

123. Don Carlos Smith, a younger brother of Joseph Smith, was a publisher of the *Times and Seasons*, a member of the city council of Nauvoo, and brigadier general of the Nauvoo Legion. He died August 7, 1841.

124. Albert P. Rockwood joined the church in Kirtland, Ohio, in 1837, gathered with the Saints in Missouri, and then settled in Nauvoo. In December 1845, he was ordained one of the First Presidents of Seventies. In 1847 Rockwood was one of the first body of pioneers to enter the Great Salt Lake Valley.

125. All commissioned officers of the Nauvoo Legion were organized by the city charter into a body referred to as a "Court Martial," with powers "to make, ordain, establish and execute all such laws and ordinances as may be considered necessary for the benefit, government, and regulation of said Legion" not inconsistent with the Constitution of the United States or of the state of Illinois. The court martial was also empowered to nominate officers for commissions or for promotions. Thus, the court martial of the Nauvoo Legion was not analogous to the usual military court martial, which is a judicial body to try military personnel accused of violations of military regulations.

126. On June 7, 1844, opponents of Joseph Smith published the first and only edition of a paper called the *Nauvoo Expositor* bitterly assailing the Mormon prophet and advocating the repeal of the Nauvoo City Charter. The Nauvoo City Council countered by declaring the *Expositor* a nuisance and ordering it abated by the city marshal with whatever help he might need from the police and the Nauvoo Legion. The order was effectively carried out June 10, 1844, but resulted in the filing of a complaint before the justice of the peace at Carthage, the county seat of Hancock County, by the publishers of the *Expositor*. Joseph and Hyrum Smith and other members of

the city council, City Marshal John P. Green, and the members of the police and Legion who had carried out the order were charged with the crime of riot allegedly committed in the destruction of the presses of the *Expositor*. Thereupon martial law was declared in Nauvoo to prevent those so charged from being arrested. Finally, on June 24, 1844, those so charged journeyed to Carthage and the following day surrendered upon being assured by Governor Thomas Ford that the State of Illinois would assure their safety. Upon the appearance of those charged with committing riot, the justice of the peace at Carthage released all of them on bail and discharged all from custody except Joseph and Hyrum Smith, who were arrested on a further charge of treason alleged to have been committed by the declaration of martial law in Nauvoo. While in jail on this new charge, Joseph and Hyrum were murdered by a mob June 27, 1844.

127. By his ordination October 4, 1844, as an elder in the quorums of seventies, Hosea was charged with the duty and authority of preaching the gospel among the nations of the earth. Seventies and members of the other orders of the priesthood in the Mormon Church are organized into bodies referred to as "quorums." Each full quorum of seventies consists of seventy members, of whom seven are chosen presidents of the quorum. The seven presidents of the first quorum preside as a council of seventies over all the other quorums and their presidents.

128. Benjamin L. Clapp had participated with Hosea and others in the Battle of Crooked River and in the flight following the battle from Missouri into Iowa and on to Illinois. He became very active in missionary work while the Saints had their headquarters at Nauvoo. In December 1845, he was named one of the presidents of the First Quorum of Seventies, but in 1859 he was excommunicated from the church.

129. Samuel Brown was one of the members of Zion's Camp in its march from Kirtland, Ohio, to Missouri in 1834, and upon his return to Kirtland he was ordained a member of the First Quorum of Seventies when the quorum was organized.

130. At this time Brigham Young held the office of president of the Council of Twelve Apostles. However, thirteen men had been ordained to the office of apostle, the thirteenth to be so ordained being Amasa M. Lyman, who was officially designated by the title of counselor to the Twelve. Lyman held the office of apostle until 1870, at which time he was excommunicated from the church for preaching false doctrine. He, together with Charles C. Rich, was one of the founders of the city of San Bernardino, California.